Light unto My Path

FORTY BIBLICAL REFLECTIONS

FR. VICTOR ABIMBOLA AMOLE

Unless otherwise noted, Scripture quotations are from the The New Jerusalem Bible ©1985.

ISBN: 978-1-4834-1206-1 (sc)
ISBN: 978-1-4834-1205-4 (e)

Library of Congress Control Number: 2014908434

Includes bibliographic references and a scriptural index

Second Revision: April 2nd, 2015.

In thanksgiving for the gift of Forty years,
Ten of those years in the priesthood

CONTENTS

FOREWORD

Christians are a people who listen and hear the Word of God. God speaks primarily and conclusively in Jesus Christ. The witness of the person and mission of Jesus is found in the gospels and letters of the New Testament.

God's word is unpredictable in its power. Beyond our own prayerful reading of the Sacred Scriptures, we all benefit from reflections on themes of the Bible to focus our understanding and to enhance the meaning, beauty and attractiveness of the message. Fr. Victor Amole has offered to us a wonderful set of reflections on the Word of God which is often described as a seed which, once sown, grows to produce fruit of grace in the hearts of men and women. This book is meant to assist the fruitful reading and reflection on the Good News.

In offering clear and engaging ways of relating to what is at the very heart of the Gospel, Father Victor is providing a real service to us who listen and hear the Word of God. His manner of writing is both pastoral and missionary in style and in purpose. The message is made accessible, while losing none of its depth and truth, and thus becomes all the more forceful and convincing.

I hope that the readers will benefit from the reflections, even as a daily meditation, to enhance their faith. I thank Father Victor for the time, energy and trust that he has invested to produce this book.

(Most Rev.) John A. Boissonneau
Auxiliary Bishop of Toronto
December, 2013

Doing the Father's will

Preach the gospel at all times. Use words if necessary
-St. Francis of Assisi

Since the beginning of known history there has been a premium placed on 'doing' as different from merely 'saying'. Jesus also supports this value, giving us that illuminating parable of the two sons. The first, being asked by the father to go into the farm and do some work, instantly said yes. But he did not go. The second, equally asked by the father to do the same work, refused. However he later thought well of it and eventually went. Jesus pointed out that the second son did the will of the father, precisely because only he did the required work.[1] Only he fulfilled the will of the father, lending credence to his words by his actions.

Thus to be a Christian in the true sense of the word is to carry out the dictates of the Father as revealed through the Son by the working of

---
[1]   Matthew 21:28-32

the Spirit. Worshiping the Father in truth and in spirit is only possible in a commitment to what he has laid down as his will; rooting for the kingdom of God to come is therefore by consequence a constant abiding, even if gradually, by the divine will. That is clear enough.

There is, however, a grey area to the understanding of this "will of the Father." The problem in our multicultural, hyper-religious world is an interpretation of what constitutes this divine will. There are several arguments in several quarters as to what is right. There are many who hold, in contrast to classical thoughts of individuals like Thomas Aquinas or even contemporary thoughts of seasoned scholars like Servais Pinckaers or William May, that there are no moral absolutes. In other words, we can always find a reason to excuse the contravention of a given natural law no matter how important such a law is. The bottom line of that argument is that situations are basically dependent on circumstances; nothing is objectively wrong or right. It is all about how it all happened and under what situation it did happen. With such an ethical stance, no law can be applied on its face value without thinking of the existent situation of the people to which it applies. And that is understandable enough.

However the logical consequence of this reasoning is a multiplication of situations which resemble more of moral dilemmas without any tangible direction as far as such situations are concerned. The question therefore surfaces again, "What is the will of the Father?" And how do we interpret such a will which is revealed to us in the Scriptures and the Sacred Tradition?[2] In the midst of the global confusion about moral issues, particularly within the sexuality ambience, what direction is to be followed?

Those questions are easier asked than answered. In these days, the will of the Father would seem difficult to discern in the light of the many troubling questions arising from a society which has grown essentially

---

2   Great sources which flow from the same divine well-spring. See *Dei Verbum*, 9.

PREFACE

For if, as Paul says, Christ is the power of God and the
wisdom of God, and if the man who does not know
Scripture does not know the power and wisdom of God,
then ignorance of Scripture is ignorance of Christ.

-St. Jerome

The observation of the writer of the second letter to Timothy
(traditionally ascribed to Paul) about the suitability of the scriptures
"for guiding people's lives and teaching them to be upright"[1] is as
correct today as it was two thousand years ago. The Word of God is
rich in all ramifications and adequately addresses life situations till
date.

The reflections in this book are essentially biblical, drawing
inspiration from forty out of the several themes which run through
the scriptures. Since the scriptures, over the last two thousand years,
have been subject of discussions and analysis, they have permeated the
society cutting across cultures, civilizations and peoples. The result is
that many theological and literary perspectives have risen over time,
springing from the living streams of the Word of God. Ample recourse
has been made to these resources in *Light Unto My Path* in order to
suitably amplify forty biblical themes and drive their messages home.
But much more, the central focus of the author is a dedicated attempt

---

[1]   1 Timothy 3:16.

at making a simple yet systematic and practical exposition of biblical themes with the intention of making their precious wealth readily available for the spiritual enrichment of readers.

The Fathers of the Vatican Council rightly noted that "Sacred tradition and Sacred Scripture form one sacred deposit of the word of God."[2] These forty reflections are written from this point of view, to "fan into a flame" the precious faith with which we have been blessed by the preaching of the apostles. A vibrant reflection on biblical themes invariably leads us to a reflection on the faith of the Church and that of her children.

Our faith teaches us that Christ Jesus is the Lord of history in whom the scriptures find their ultimate fulfilment. He is the "joy of man's desiring", the fulfilment of the Old Testament and the crown of the New Testament. Taking time to do some lively reflection on the scriptures is therefore ultimately turning to Jesus, the saving Lord of history, in whom all preoccupations or worries find an answer.

A number of people have been quite helpful in realizing this publication. I seize the opportunity here to thank them all. I am grateful to Bishop John Boissonneau for reading through this work and graciously taking the time to write its' foreword. My immense gratitude to Msgr. J.K.A. Aniagwu, Prof. Andrzej S. Wodka and Prof. Nuria Calduch-Benages, Lou Iacobelli and Giuseppina Pappalardo for their reviews and endorsements. I particularly thank Frs. Joseph Akanbi, Francis Adelabu and Felix Adedigba for their suggestions and contributions. My immediate family members and innumerable number of friends and colleagues have formed an intricate web of friendship and love which has really enriched me. Such an enrichment naturally produces different fruits at different seasons, one of them evidenced by this production. From the home front in Ibadan, to the

---

2   II Vatican Council, Dogmatic Constitution on Divine Revelation, *Dei Verbum*, 10

home from home in Canada and Italy, I wish to say am grateful to you all for your beautiful roles in my life.

It is my sincere hope that these reflections will stimulate some fervour of doing more mediation on the living words of the scriptures, the knowledge of which is the knowledge of Christ.

Rev. Fr. Victor Abimbola Amole
December 6, 2013

self-referent. The situation becomes more compounded when we realize that the definition of that institution which is usually regarded as the better source of interpretation of the Father's will, the Church of God, is today far from being lucid. The different groups within the body of Christ, represented in different ecclesial communities, lay claim to different understanding of the Father's will. The scourge of disunity therefore complicates further an already difficult moral horizon. This has made for the disparate interpretation of the "will of the Father."

In the face of this sort of dilemma and difficulty, it is important to remind ourselves that the early moments of the Church as a united body of Christ were never quite free of such moral quagmires. Take for instance a major difficulty which the early church, as administered by the apostles, faced: the issue of deciding the necessity or otherwise of circumcision.[3] While the gentile converts wanted freedom from this practice, the Jewish converts would not hear of neglecting their valued culture and religious practice. It is easy for us to read this as mere history now, but it was a real moral dilemma for those early witnesses of faith.

As it was in the beginning, so it is now. The Church of God rose up to this moral dilemma of circumcision by giving a rule, inspired by the Holy Spirit, not to burden gentile converts with the obligation of circumcision. That of course could not have been satisfactory to all parties, particularly the zealous Jewish converts. But that was the outcome of the deliberation of the Church, inspired by the Holy Spirit. And by the way, this rule of exception, given by the Apostles and elders in the Church in Jerusalem, became the proceeding of the first ever Council in the Church.[4] The point here is that there is yet the moral

---

[3]   See Acts of Apostles 15:5-29

[4]   A foundational step towards what would eventually become Ecumenical Councils in the Church. See Leo Donald Davis, The First Seven Ecumenical Councils, (Minnesota: Liturgical Press, 1990), pp. 21ff.

voice of Christ speaking through his Church, even in the midst of a cacophony of several views.

That "still voice" does not cease to make its direction known in the guidance it gives to the Church of Christ even today. Moral dilemmas therefore may never end. But the will of the Father would always be made known in that "still voice", which ever animates the Church of Christ as she navigates the turbulent waters of history.

"Doing the Father's will" in our pluralistic society and religiously-divided world would always have to pass the moral crucible of deciphering "what is the Father's will?", a question which cannot possibly receive a consensual answer in the society. It is for such moral crucibles as this that Christ has set up his Church "to teach all nations", not basing her convictions on human reasoning or some popular consensus, but on the directions of He who has promised to be with his Church "to the end of time."[5]

---

5   Matthew 28:19-20

Do not be Afraid

Say to the faint hearted 'Be strong! Do not be afraid.'

-Isaiah 35:3

John Paul II's pontificate would always be remembered in the annals of history. Right from the very homily of his inauguration in 1978, the man of God had set a tone for his papacy and the courageous witness he was bringing in for the faithful. His refrain at that inauguration was "Do not be afraid." Little did he know that those words would eventually accompany his ministry as he led the Church of Christ for almost three decades, lending his voice not only to evangelization causes all over the world but to many initiatives that promoted the emancipation of peoples from all sorts of shackles.

"Do not be afraid." We experience several causes of fear in our lives. The society in which we live overwhelms us often with its demands and burdens. Life's journey, desirable as we would want it to be, is often not quite straight, coming at us with its jolts and shocks. Were things left

5

to our own plans and orderings maybe this might not bother us as such, for we would do all in our power to order our days in peace. But often the scheme of things goes beyond our commands and we sometimes become almost helpless. The best of plans and future arrangement sometimes come crumbling in a day, with just one setback of life. Indeed, as it is said, "events mock at human foresight, nothing is certain as the unforeseen." In the events of such circumstances as painted here, what becomes the response of a Christian? How does he go on adhering to values? How does she cope with the so demanding constraints of life and their somewhat fearful consequences?

The history of the people of God in the scriptures is a beautiful illustration of God's support and care especially at times of fear and delusion. Their experiences call the Christian to a "lifting up of the head" for our helper is the Lord of Israel. For instance, the exilic experience of God's people in Babylon was a cause for concern and fear. There was hardly anything more to hope for, the people's heart had waned with fear. But the voice of Isaiah the prophet was never silent in giving the people admonitions of courage and challenging them not to be afraid. His main argument was that there was nothing God could not accomplish. He would make water gush in the desert and streams in the wastelands. He would rescue his people and resettle them in their own lands amidst joy and gladness. Indeed, the prophecy of Isaiah came to pass; the people of God got their liberty from Babylon.

Fear could be so crippling that it prevents us from seeing the possibility of a bright future. The shadow of the present can so oppress our sight that it limits our vision of lights in the surroundings beyond the shadow. But a message like that of Isaiah brings relief to our hearts. There is nothing beyond the power of the omnipotent. Nothing is beyond the power of God. Belligerent as fear could be therefore, the Christian must learn to confront its ferocious challenge with a sturdy lance of courage, hope and trust.

Reflecting on the crippling effect of fear and the need to shatter its bastions, it is equally important to remember our call to solidarity in facing fear and arduous times. By virtue of our baptism, we are called not only to resist fear and trust in the saving power of Yeshua[1] but also to lend courage to others when their faith is weak. Learning from the very symbol of our faith, the Christian person is a being of hope for whom such an image of hopelessness, torture and death as the cross becomes a symbol of hope, life and redemption. No fear is therefore enough to conquer the courage of the Christian or prevent him from giving a hand of help when the reality of fear threatens the brethren.

In the face of the menace of hopelessness, fear, sorrow, needs, sickness and anxiety, we are called to remember from where the Christian victory emerges. Right from the cross, the least place imaginable since ordinarily it is an instrument of fear. But in the hands of the saviour it has become a source of solace, salvation and peace. As John Paul reminds us, "the power of Christ's Cross and Resurrection is greater than any evil which man could or should fear."[2]

Therefore do not be afraid of that seemingly fearful reality. It is not a reality bigger than death. And that bigger reality Christ already conquered.

---

[1]   Hebraic corresponding version of the Greek name *Iesous* "Jesus". It is usually translated as "the Lord saves", apparently a reference to Matthew 1:21, "She will give birth to a son and you must name him Jesus, because he is the one who is to save his people from their sins."

[2]   John Paul II, *Crossing the Threshold of Hope*, (New York: Alfred Knopf Inc., 1994) p. 219.

3

The Lord who Feeds us with His Life

If angels could be jealous of men, they would be so for one reason: Holy Communion.

-St. Maximillan Kolbe

The mystery of Corpus Christi, (Corpus et Sanguis Christi or The Body and Blood of Christ) is one of the most important of all the mysteries of faith which we hold so dear in the Catholic faith. It is the mystery of the body, blood, soul and divinity of our Lord, his complete being given to us "in order to perpetuate the sacrifice of the cross throughout the ages until he should come again, and so to entrust to his beloved Spouse, the Church, a memorial of his death and resurrection: a sacrament of love, a sign of unity, a bond of charity, a Paschal banquet in which Christ is consumed, the mind is filled with grace, and a pledge of future glory is given to us."[1]

This beautiful yet mysterious reality often calls our human and therefore rational mind to a deep wonder. How could this be? What actually is the divine presence? How could Jesus feed us with his body and blood? It is natural for those thoughts to arise in our hearts sometimes. They are not necessarily questions of doubt but thoughts seeking a direction, faith seeking understanding, humanity seeking to enter into a perception of a sublime, divine mystery. The Jews who were the direct recipients of this mystery had also wondered at "these sayings" of Jesus, arguing among themselves and asking "how can this man give us his flesh to eat?"[2] The interesting dimension to that story is that Jesus did not recant on that 'weird' teaching but insists "in all truth I tell you, if you do not eat the flesh of the Son of man and drink his blood, you have no life in you."[3] Indeed, when many of his disciples left him after hearing this controversial call to eating his body, he simply asked his apostles if they too would like to go! He would not budge on his teaching, even at the cost of losing his close collaborators. Thank God they stayed, and by their ministry and preaching, we have the gift of the Holy Eucharist in the Church today.

Jesus teaches that no one has a greater love, than to lay down his life for his friends.[4] It is in the mystery of the *Corpus Christi* that he wished to manifest the whole of his love for humanity. That same body and blood, which would be sacrificed on Golgotha two days later, he gave to us at the Last Supper to keep as his memorial for all time to come. But not just as a memorial, but as a feast which nourishes us and communicates life to us. In this sacred sacrament we have a truly unique encounter with Christ who forms us and prepares us to face the

---

[1]   The Code of Canon Law, 1323.
[2]   John 6:52
[3]   John 6:53
[4]   John 15:13

demands of our daily existence. Archbishop Fulton Sheen would say "as a man must be born before he can begin to lead his physical life, so he must be born to lead a Divine Life. That birth occurs in the Sacrament of Baptism. To survive, he must be nourished by Divine Life; that is done in the Sacrament of the Holy Eucharist."[5] This food of angels given to us mortals is therefore a fortification for our spirit and our body. It is truly the bread of life descended from heaven, the mystery of our faith, medicine of immortality.[6] In the sacrament of the body and blood of Christ, we have the source of all the sacraments. Understood in this light, it is no surprise that the Eucharist has been aptly described by the Church as "the source and summit of the Christian life."[7]

How could we possibly and adequately value such a gracious gift? Perhaps with a greater attention to the presence of the King in his temple, the Lord on his throne, God in the tabernacle, we could draw nearer to the depth of the divine mysteries. Perhaps we could step into a church which we would ordinarily pass by now and then and have a chat with He who is humble enough to reside in a wafer. And you know what? It is not surprising that he decided to perpetuate his presence in this manner. Looking at his mode of appearance on earth as a little and vulnerable babe in swaddling clothes, it is no shock that he decided to perpetuate his presence amongst us in the form of bread and wine.

Just go to him. Pass by and say hi! He has not ceased to surprise his own. He would enter into your situation and leave you with a 'wow!' experience.

Taste and see that the Lord is good.

---

[5]   Archbishop Fulton Sheen, *The Eucharist*, *Audio Book on CD*,(Greenville, Texas: Casscom Media, May 1, 2013).

[6]   See the Litany of the Blessed Sacrament

[7]   *Lumen Gentium*, 11.

The Most Holy Trinity

Firmly I believe and truly
God is three, and God is one
And I next acknowledge duly
Manhood taken by the Son.

The story is told of the Parish Priest who, in the company of his assistant, was visiting a senior kindergarten class of the parish school next door. It was the Monday just after the Holy Trinity Sunday. Wanting to use the opportunity to catechise the kids about the reality of the Holy Trinity he asked "who can tell me what the Blessed Trinity means?" A little girl lisped, "The Blethed Twinity meanth there are thwee perthonth in one God." The priest, gladdened by the great enthusiasm of the kid, requested "Would you say that again please? I don't understand what you said." The little girl answered, "Y'not thuppothed to underthtand; 't'th a mythtewy." The priest admitted to his assistant later on "you know, that little girl got me catechised!"

The doctrine of the Holy Trinity is surely one of the most difficult if not about the mostdifficult doctrine of the Christian faith. One can appreciate why: it is a doctrine by which men seek to explain the nature of God. Though there are indications in the scriptures as to the doctrine of the Trinity[1], there is no explicit teaching in the entire scripture to categorically point out the mystery of one God living in three persons. The sacred tradition which the Church received from the apostles has however always treasured the doctrine of the Trinity. It was definitively proclaimed as a doctrine at the Council of Nicaea (AD 325). And since this solemn proclamation, several Fathers of the Church have laboured to explain the doctrine using different symbols. Of this, St. Augustine would seem most popular.

Exemplary men and women, now called saints, have also tried to give us aids towards better appreciating this mystery. St. Patrick used the tripartite leaf of the shamrock to illustrate a more unintelligible reality. St. Cyril used the symbol of the sun with its glorious blaze, the light it gives, and the heat that it produces to illustrate same. St. John Mary Vianney tried to illustrate the mystery of the Holy Trinity with the symbols of candlelight and a rose. The flame from candlelight has colour, warmth and shape but the three are expressions of the same flame. A rose has colour, fragrance and shape but always the expressions of the same rose.

---

[1] Biblical scholars point to the pluralistic language at creation, "let us form man in our own image" (Genesis 1:26); Yahweh's visitation to Abraham in the form of three angels (Genesis 18:2, an experience which is actually celebrated by the Russian Orthodox Church as "Abraham's Trinitarian experience"). In the New Testament there are allusions to the Trinity in the descent of the Holy Spirit upon Jesus at his Baptism and the sound of the voice of the Father (Matthew 3:16-17); the great commission of Christ to his disciples to preach the good news and baptize them in the name of the Father and of the Son, and of the Holy Spirit" (John 10:30); Paul's Trinitarian greeting format in 2 Corinthians 13:14; indications from the universal letters of 1 Peter 1:2-3a and St. John 1 john 5:5-6.

However, no matter the fineness of the thoughts and the intelligence used in explaining this mystery, the truth remains that it is a mystery. The best of human logic cannot explain a divine mystery. It is an article of faith passed on and received in tradition. Hence it is not just a matter of what language is used to attempt unraveling this mystery, or what intense study is put into such attempt. For instance, these days a sexist pluralism has arisen even in the discourse about the nature of God, referring to God as a She and not a He. The truth remains that all these arguments on which pronoun is appropriate to qualify God would always be inadequate since they aim at comprehending the divine in anthropomorphic (human) terms.

Be that as it may, for us Christians who receive this article of faith in humility and simplicity, it is by itself a whole lesson to the life to which we are called. In imitation of the most Holy Trinity, God calls us to unity and oneness. The several races, tongues, peoples and cultures of the world are but manifestation of a great God who lives in unity, a God who calls us to an understanding of our differences as a blessing. Diversity is positive. And as the Holy Father Francis rightly puts it recently, the strive to achieve uniformity at all cost often erodes the presence of the Spirit amongst us.[2] The beauty of our creation and the wonder of our being lie in the diversity which we bear, as individuals and as groups, shared with us all by a triune God, purely out of love.

And may the grace of our Lord Jesus Christ, the love of God and the fellowship of the Holy Spirit remain with us.

---

[2] See the message of the General Papal Audience, Saint Peter's Square Rome, Wednesday, October 9, 2013.

Even that Little is Enough

This lil' light of mine, I'm gonna let it shine} 3x
Let it shine, shine, shine, Let it shine!

The song above is reputed to have been written by a white pastor for children of black slaves as a source of inspiration, a reminder that there is no limit to what these little ones could achieve in spite of the then apparent gloomy socio-cultural challenges. Their light indeed seemed to be little, very slim chances at a good life, very bad social conditions. But even that little was enough, for it was like a wood touched by the little spark of life. It was enough to become a real ember. For where there is life, there exists an abundance of hope and possibilities.

Today, several millions of those children of slave parents are big names and personalities. The song has proved to be true, taken over by several musicians who have made varying renditions of it. But the sheer force of its words has not ceased to amaze me. "This little light of mine…"; the concept of little; the concept of what can be achieved with the supposedly little.

There are two miracles in the gospel that beautifully illustrate what can be done with apparently little things. Biblical theologians often refer to these miracles as Eucharistic because of their food-based theme. The first is the Old Testament account of the multiplication of flour and oil by the prophet Elijah. It was a time of famine. In spite of an obvious situation of the proximity of starvation, a widow had courageously prepared some food for Elijah from her last 'handful of meal' and 'little oil'. The point here is that the widow made use of the little she had, gave it away in faith, and this little became a source of plenty all through the time of famine. "The jar of meal was not spent nor the jug of oil emptied, just as Yahweh had foretold through Elijah."[1]

The second miracle was by our Lord. He had been preaching to the people "and when evening came the disciples went to him and said, 'this is a lonely place, and time has slipped by; so send the people away, and they can go to the villages to buy themselves some food.' "[2] The disciples must have realized there was no way of feeding these people, "five thousand men to say nothing of women and children", without dispersing them to nearby villages. But of course there was a way for He who is the Way. Asking if there was nothing the disciples could do to feed the people without having to send them away they replied, "All we have with us is five loaves and two fish", intending to show what a drop that would seem like in the ocean of people before them. But it was enough for the Way to carve a way round the situation. The people were fed and there were twelve baskets full of scraps left over.

Now that is a miracle, the power of the little becoming so much as to create left-overs. C. S. Lewis defines a miracle as "a retelling in small letters of the very same story which is written across the whole world

---

[1] I King 17: 1-16
[2] Matthew 14:15ff

in letters too large for some of us to see."[3] We all have these miracles of "little" stuff in our hands. We have the miracle of that little light which indeed, if given enough care, can shine bright. We all have some "five loaves" and "two fish" which can feed a multitude.

St. Theresa of Lisieux is popularly called Theresa of the little flower not only because she loved flowers but because she did her things in little ways yet creating big effects. Though she died when she was only 24, she is one of the four women-Doctors of the Church alongside St. Catherine of Sienna, St. Teresa of Avila and St. Hildegard of Bingen. Mother Teresa of Calcutta too was a woman of the same virtue. She rendered her little parts and it became a little light that shone quite far, nourishing millions from the famine of care and love, the real cause of famine. Her impact was felt all around the globe.

That little is enough for you to start with. What is that goal of yours which seems so far and unreachable? What is your dream that seemed light years away from possibility? The little you have now is enough. Start with that and the Lord of harvest will give increase to the apparent little.

Let us pray with the apostles and say "Lord increase our faith." And He would answer, "If you had faith like a mustard seed..."[4] That little is good enough to get you started.

---

[3] C. S. Lewis, *God in the Dock: Essays on Theology and Ethics*, (Grand Rapids, Michigan: Eerdmans Publishing Co, 1994), p. 29.

[4] Luke 17: 6

6

Suffering

Great achievement is usually born of great sacrifice, and is never the result of selfishness.

-Napoleon Hill

The human person, even though essentially rational, is also a being of senses. Pleasure and pain are important dimensions of our lives. Often to the extent to which we experience pleasure, to that extent we tend to measure our contentment. As a matter of fact often pleasure becomes not just a measure of contentment for us but a measure of happiness, even though in essence pleasure is quite far from what it means to be happy.

On the other hand suffering naturally brings us a negativity feeling. It is an experience which we try as much as possible to keep at bay. It is almost seen as incompatible with our quest for joy and happiness. Yet the Lord teaches us nothing could be as wrong as this notion of separating human fulfilment and joy from vulnerability, from an openness to suffering. Indeed he says those disturbing words "if anyone wants to be a follower of mine, let him renounce himself and take up his cross and follow me."[1] On this account, Christianity has often been rejected by several as a *kill-joy*. And for us who are Christians, we somewhat find ourselves struggling with the concept of suffering and the multi-headed questions of pain and sacrifice.

The teaching of Jesus is however insightful on suffering. When he says "unless you take up your cross and follow me, you cannot be my disciple", he does not leave this condition just by itself. He provides the motif for such a statement. "Anyone who wants to save his life will lose it; but anyone who loses his life for my sake will find it." This is even more disturbing. If you love someone, why would you wish suffering for same? Yet Jesus' teaching is full of wisdom. Even though this teaching is meant to stimulate a deep spiritual life which understands the mission of the "Son of man" who has come to suffer and by the virtue of this suffering save humanity, it is also a lesson meant to recall our attention to our human nature.

From a simple observation of daily occurrences and our simple experiences, we realize that nothing good is hardly achieved without some sacrifice; nothing worthy comes by without some pain. The student burns the proverbial midnight candle to achieve success, and the more he exerts himself at being committed to that study, the more his chances of excellence. The athlete gives all she can to her practices and drills, and the more she rigorously devotes attention to these painful practices and exercises the more fit she becomes and, by consequence, the more chances she has at laurels. The truly professional, even when he has already made his name, never stops working at excellence and doing everything to maintain the status of that name.

Now if all these are true of the connection between excellence and sacrifices, how much more is the wisdom in the lesson that Jesus meant to transmit to us about the immense value of Christian sacrifice?

---

[1]   Matthew 16:24

Seen in this light the Cross, ordinarily a symbol of torture and agony, becomes a powerful emblem of victory just as we have come to experience it in the life of Jesus. The Cross was to be the end of him, it indeed made him. The Lord puts it to us that those difficulties are necessary to make us; they are pathways to becoming the better "us"; our golden self comes out refined and glamorous when it passes through the kiln of discomfort and sacrifice.

It is true, sometimes the experience of the cross and sacrifice is so big in some individual circumstances. There may be some disease to cope with, a death of a young one, some catastrophe of some kind. These are not experiences easy to write away. But one thing is sure: neither was it easy to comprehend the Cross of Christ. The apostles as a matter of fact rejected it, so much so that Peter was called the devil.[2] The fact that Christians preach a crucified Christ seems most ridiculous. Yet in that ridicule abides the fullness of the power of God who saves in weakness and pain.

---

[2]   Matthew 16:23

Go and Sin no more

I made my sin known to you, did not conceal my guilt. I said, 'I shall confess my offence to Yahweh.' And you for your part, took away my guilt

-Psalm 32:5

John Paul II was one of the most famous Popes of our time. He was famous not only because of his nearness to the people and his many travels but also because of his several writings, covering wide areas of human life and ministering in a most meaningful way to many. In 1984 he wrote an Apostolic Exhortation which he titled Reconciliation and Penance, focusing on the mystery of sin. One of the sub-themes of that writing was the loss of the sense of sin in our world; the fact that sin is hardly even recognized any more. Indeed as a Yoruba proverb says, "a city that has no laws has no crime."[1] If sin is not even as much as recognized, well then nothing is ever wrong. All is well.

---

[1]   "Ìlu tí ò s'ófin, èsè ò sí níbè."

But we know all is not well. The reality of sin strikes us in the face everywhere: in the tears of relatives of a murdered person; in the agony of those who have suffered some scam or the other; in the licentious lifestyle and low morals of contemporary life; in the lies, deception and pretence that abound; in the varied forms of the promotion of the culture of death; in the private court of our individual consciences.

In a larger dimension, our shattered world reveals the grotesque faces of sin in the trampling upon human rights and freedom, various forms of discrimination, violence and terrorism, stockpiling of war weapons, unjust distribution of world recourses.[2] No, the reality of sin is well established in our midst. What is often obscure is the sense of it.

The pain is that sin and its discomforting consequences cannot be taken away without human beings who are agents of moral or immoral actions acknowledging same and working at it. The Holy book says "If my people who bear my name humble themselves, and pray and seek my presence and turn from their wicked ways, then I will listen from heaven and forgive their sins and restore their country."[3] There is no forgiveness, nor remedy, nor healing without acknowledgement and repentance.

The good news is that the Lord is ever inviting us to repentance. That symbolic Father of the prodigal son is ever waiting by the door. The deceit of sin sometimes is that it is too weighty to be forgiven but God says "though your sins are like scarlet, they shall be white as snow; though they are red as crimson, they shall be like wool."[4] Or sometimes the deceit is "there is no sense in trying any more, I'll go back to the same sin right after." But good sense tells us we do not believe this manner of reasoning usually. When we do not do well in an exam, or when an athlete performs woefully, or when we trip and fall down on the ground, we do not say "there is no sense in trying again; there is

---

2   John Paul II, *Reconciliation and Penance*, (1984), no. 2.

3   1 Chronicles 7:14

4   Isaiah 1:18

no sense in standing up since it would happen again!" No, we do not. We stand up, try again, prepare ourselves, and try again and again. It is the lie of the evil one to ensnare the mind to believe that sin is always repeated and so need not be lamented. It is a snare to keep moral development at bay.

The Lord speaks to each and every conscience to realize that which has been done wrong, call it by its name, repent of it and be healed. Painting wrong acts as okay or the usage of euphemism cannot help us to overcome sins. The story of the young man who went to the priest and confessed stealing a rope without mentioning he equally dragged away the cow tethered to the end of the rope is incredible. But it is revealing of what we do when we cover sins and wrongs.

We could not wish for a more merciful Lord. He has given several assurances that his mercy endures forever. He challenged authorities in his days, asking for a greater exercise of mercy and pardon. He risked his life, pardoning offenders and mingling with so called sinners. Indeed, he died in the midst of two criminals readily pardoning one who recognized his sins and asked for salvation.

May we too experience the liberating joy of pardon. But first, may we have the moral strength to recognize our wrongs and seek forgiveness.

8

$\mathcal{F}$reedom

Man is born free, and everywhere he is in chains.

-Jean-Jacques Rousseau

Martin Luther, a vibrant theologian and a very conscientious German priest of the 16th century (November 10, 1483 - February 18, 1546) led the Protestant Reformation. He had perceived some lack in the ecclesiastical administration and doctrinal formations of his day and made a move for a change. There were however some points in which Luther was not necessarily right. One of such is in the debates on freedom/liberty and the law. Taking his cue from Paul[1], Luther had claimed that Christians are free from the law since they are justified by faith alone and led by the Spirit. In his words, "it is clear then that to a Christian man his faith suffices for everything, and that he has no need of works for justification. But if he has no need of works, neither has he need of the law; and, if he has no need of the law, he is certainly

---

[1]   Galatians 5:18

23

free from the law."[2] His contention was against the scholastic teaching which encouraged good works. The Church pronounced Luther's position as an error and reiterated there should not be a dichotomy in the Christian's recognition of grace in his life, even as he should be aware of the necessity of good works. Thank God there have been good attempts towards better understanding between Lutherans and the mother Church today, and tremendous moves towards greater unity for which Christ prayed.

Freedom is indeed a beautiful gift of God. It is in fact argued as the greatest gift after life itself. Many great thinkers have argued that rationality, often seen as the hallmark of the human person, is not as important as the gift and possibility of freedom. That argument is more than persuasive. Rationality helps us to perceive, think and to choose, but what if there was even no freedom to choose at all?

The joy of freedom is boundless. Ranging from the simple freedom to choose to eat rice instead of pasta or the other way round; to choose to wear a favourite brown skirt or knot a red tie; to choose to watch a comedy or a gripping thriller. Then to the more comprehensive understanding of freedom in the sense of being able to choose to become an Administrative Secretary, or a Medical Doctor or an Engineer or a Priest; the freedom to choose to marry this lady or this man and not that other one. The freedom to choose, the freedom to be. What if there was no freedom? The answer to that question can hardly be imagined without some cringing. Though some people argue that Adam should not have had the freedom which brought us the consequence of the original sin, yet the freedom which caused this "happy fault" of Adam would hardly be given up by such people. The truth is that God shared with us of his nature, of his liberty, of his fullness. He created us to be free.

---

2   Martin Luther, *Concerning Christian Liberty*, 22, in *The Harvard Classics*, ed. Charles Elliot, (New York: P.F. Collier and Son, 1909-14).

However, to whom much is given even much more is expected. The awesome gift of freedom calls us to a great responsibility. Often the shirking of that responsibility comes with grave consequences. For instance people suffer when we misuse our freedom; there is a lot of hurt when proper responsibility is not considered in the use of freedom. More than this, we too suffer a lot when this beautiful freedom is not responsibly used as is evident in the cases of drunk driving, waste of time, uncontrolled cravings, etc.

In trying to help the Galatians put the gift of freedom in proper perspective and use, St. Paul exhorted,

> Brothers, you were called to be free; do not use your freedom as an opening for self-indulgence, but be servants to one another in love, since the whole of the law is summarised in the one commandment: you must love your neighbour as yourself.[3]

Thus no true freedom aims at caging the other. Any use of freedom which does not promote even a greater freedom is suspect. Freedom is therefore not merely getting my own way or what Paul refers to as indulging myself. My freedom to drink alcohol must be able to promote my freedom to act responsibly thereafter and not as a drunk. My freedom to listen to music must promote your freedom to enjoy tranquillity and serenity, and thus calls for a responsibility on my part. To make it simple and pragmatic, Paul calls this responsibility part "love". And indeed that is what it is. For love is not just some wilful thinking, but a responsible choice of the good of the other person.

Let us bask in our God-given freedom, giving thanks to the source of all freedom, the Lord who sets us free to live responsibly.

---

[3] Galatians 5: 13-14

To Nurture or be Nurtured

If you see charity, you see the Trinity
Augustine, De Trinitate, VIII, 8, 12: CCL 50, 287

The biblical figures of Martha and Mary, the sisters of Lazarus, are prominent for the average Christian. In the story recounted by the evangelist Luke these two sisters seem to represent the faces of hospitality and discipleship respectively.[1] They appear as symbols of arguments regarding the importance of nurturing on the one hand, or being nurtured on the other. On a certain occasion that Jesus was on a visit to the sisters' house, Martha got all busy with entertaining him as any good host would. Mary however simply sat at his feet, literarily glued to the words that flowed from his mouth, conversing with him and learning from the fount of wisdom.

In several Christian discourses these two apparently opposed behaviours of the two sisters of Lazarus have received different

---

[1]   Luke 10:38-42

evaluations. While some argue that Martha's care for the visiting master was appropriate, many others oppose a flight after material preoccupations while ignoring the source of all good in the person of Jesus. And the last argument often seems to have the upper hand as Jesus himself had lauded Mary's choice as the best.

The question I often ask myself on reflecting on this dilemma of a seeming oscillation between nurturing like Martha or being nurtured like Mary is "did Jesus eat of the food that Martha was preparing at the end of his discourse with Mary?" Answer that question and you will not but have a strong urge to laugh. I would say he must have. He came to be entertained anyway; he was a visitor. Knowing him from the way He is presented in the scriptural accounts, Jesus was a homely, social person. The gospels had made reference to him as the son of man who "came eating and drinking."[2] So what do you think? Jesus condemns Martha as running about while he commends Mary as having chosen the better part only to turn around to feast on Martha's food? Oh yes that seems to be the case, hilarious as it may sound!

This turning around to feast on Martha's food however shifts our focus somewhat, making us see Jesus' take on the dilemma in a more lucid manner. He was surely not condemning the act of nurturing. Hospitality is a Christian gesture, and Jesus himself had encouraged at different instances in the scriptures the importance of being hospitable and kind. His presence at different dinners and feasts underscores the point. At a point in time he even invited himself to Zacchaeus' house.

Rather the point of Jesus at the sisters' house is an opening of the eyes to the primary while not forgetting the secondary. It is not so much the lauding of Mary as a listener while condemning Martha as a busybody, but the presentation of values in their proper order. If Jesus is the fullness of all good and in him inheres all virtues, there is no doubt all hospitality and all nurturing flows from him. Thus while Mary is lauded because she sat at the master's feet learning and

---

[2]   Matthew 11:19; Luke 7:34

drinking from this source of hospitality, the learning period or this period of being nurtured must have to come to an end and then flow into another important period in time: the nurturing period. There is no true listening to the Word that ends at listening. The Word is always heard in order to consequently galvanize us into action. We refer to that as 'bearing fruit' in the gospel language.

Thus even Mary, who is here lauded, would eventually have to arise from being nurtured and go nurture, from listening to doing, from taking to giving. True Christian charity begins from a learning of what charity means. It begins from an alignment with Charity itself; it begins with being formed in the school of the master. Schooling at the master's feet is however ridiculously useless if the student would not eventually act on the knowledge gained, like the true scribe who becomes a disciple and, having being taught, "brings out from his storeroom new things as well as old." The one who is truly nurtured learns to emerge from the gift of being nurtured to the field of nurturing.

This again is one of the lessons of Jesus to the twelve on the evening before he suffered. He washed their feet individually. It is a sweet experience to be pampered, cared for, nurtured, and taught. But he says to them, "I have given you an example so that you may copy what I have done to you."[3] The ultimate desire and obligation of a Christian is to nurture after being nurtured.

---

[3] John 13:15

Prayer: Remaining Grafted to the Vine

You don't know how to pray? Put yourself in the presence of God, and as soon as you have said, 'Lord, I don't know how to pray!" you can be sure you have already begun. - St. Josemaria Escriva, *The Way*, 90

A sentence in the lyrics of one Nigerian song literally translates as "prayer is the walking stick with which we journey with God." This is a simple but pragmatic symbolism. God is spirit and all those who walk with him must do so in the spirit. That prayer is important for the Christian is never in doubt. The challenge often is being so convinced of its importance as to begin to pray. This challenge sometimes branches off into two: the lethargy which often corrodes the Christian fervor to pray and the "how" to pray.

But let us look at it this way. Suppose we simply define prayer as a communication? Prayer is a communication with God. That is simplistic but most revealing of the role prayer is meant to play in the life of the Christian. To be human is to communicate, for the bond of humanity flows only in the links of communication. The more robust the communication of a married couple for instance, the more robust their unity and nearness to each other. A popular story recounts the experience of an otherwise united couple who were caught up in malice because of a domestic argument. The husband was to go for an appointment the next day at 8am. But just because he was not willing to break the silence, he simply wrote a little note and placed beside the bedside of the wife, requesting her to wake him up at 7am the next day so as to be able to make his appointment. In her turn, the wife too was not willing to be the first to break the yoke of malice. At 7am she equally placed the reminder note at the bedside of the husband. Of course it goes without saying he never woke up in time for that appointment.

That is the case of a communication gone bad; a lack in the flow of what you could call "a daily bargaining of life" in which, like stepping into the same water of a lake, we touch each other's life. This communication is what we do in prayers, engaging in a relationship of dialoging with God. Prayer is not so much an obligation, some ritual necessary to please God because we are believers. It is more of a necessity, a part of the code necessary to keep us functioning and running smoothly. If Henry Ford created the Ford sedan and gave a manual as to its functionality, the best way to keep that vehicle running and good is to make constant recourse to that manual which speaks the mind of Ford and sets out easy ways to help keep the vehicle in shape. Now that is but a simplistic analogy to paint a bigger picture of our need of getting in touch with the creator on a constant basis. He does not create and leave us like some absconded God. He does not even leave us with a manual to continue to decipher the workings of our complicated selves. Rather he himself is ever available for consultation and dialogue to readily provide answers.

Now this availability is of vital importance not only to give answers in times of some malfunction or when we are in need of "information" to resolve issues, but even when there is no issue to resolve. Fulton Sheen quotes St. Augustine as saying "We may pray most when we say least, and we may pray least when we say most."[1] Thus prayer is not about the much talk or several intentions. It is a passing of time with God in whom we live, move and have our being.[2] It is a getting to know more of ourselves even as we know of him.

The lives of great men and women who have successfully tapped into a dedicated communication with God instruct us about the wisdom of doing same. Archbishop Fulton Sheen was fond of talking often of his dependence on prayers.[3] When asked what the source of his eloquence was, the great man would always refer to his dependence on God. The same experience holds true for countless number of persons who have experienced grace and sustenance. They have learnt to fly on eagles wings, communicating with the source of life.

The Lord categorically makes us to understand how to bear much fruit. It is by remaining grafted to the Vine, "for cut off from me you can do nothing".[4] It is obvious, not only from the success of the several persons who have remained united to God in prayer but from the very admonition of Christ himself, that our relevance and fruitfulness reside in our keeping the communication between us and God alive in prayers.

---

[1]   See Fulton Sheen, *Wartime Prayer Book*, (Manchester: Sophia Institute Press, 2003), p. viii.

[2]   Acts of Apostles 17:28

[3]   Patricia Kossman, "Remembering Fulton Sheen", *America*, (December 6, 2004), 10.

[4]   John 15:5

Just One Source of Joy

Joy in Christ requires a commitment to working at the Christian lifestyle. Salvation comes as a gift, but the joy of salvation demands disciplined action. Most Christians I know have just enough of the Gospel to make them miserable, but not enough to make them joyful.

- Tony Campolo, *Seven Deadly Sins*

The wise man who wrote the book of Ecclesiastes must have been a deep thinker, and one with a sense of humour too. In one of his musings he wondered about the ridiculous pattern of existence that man experiences in life only to abandon all. "Vanity of vanities" the preacher called it. Apparently this author must have ruminated on the immense stress to which man person subjects himself, the uncountable duels he fights with life, and the arduous efforts he makes to achieve a goal. But once achieved, this goal only sets a tone for the beginning of yet another struggle to attain a different goal. Seemingly, the human person appears insatiable; or rather, maybe it is better to say the choices we make in the bid of satisfying ourselves appear futile.

The Lord Jesus, in responding to a preoccupation of this same type had proposed a parable as to what gives man lasting joy. The parable is often called "the parable of the rich fool"[1] It recounts the story of a wealthy man who did all that was possible to make provision for himself and his future, but only to lose all the very night he thought he was to sit down, relax and begin enjoying it all. Again it opens the mind to the vanity of it all. This man did all well, fought the good fight of life, worked diligently and as much as the scriptures tell us, did all this within the confines of virtues. But what was lacking, why was he to suffer the loss of it all if the only fault he had was to have worked hard?

The point of the Lord in the parable was to show the falsity of reposing hope for lasting joy and contentment in the work of our hands or in the pursuit of our imagination. Storing up all sorts of treasure to assure ourselves of joy and peace amounts to nothing if the only source of joy and contentment is ignored. And Jesus says that singular source is God, for it is mere futility "...for anyone to win the whole world and forfeit his life."[2]

Again, as in many instances in the scriptures, material wealth is not what is being condemned here. In fact, I find meaningful that popular comment which is often credited to a famous ecclesiastic, "the Church is not built on Hail Marys alone." He had meant to communicate the importance of generosity and the necessity of supporting the cause of evangelization with material wealth. And I guess you can only be generous with what you have! Thus wealth itself is not the problem. The point in question therefore is a rediscovering of the proper position of wealth and an understanding that it does not give much joy if the only source of joy is absent.

---

[1] Luke 12:13-21
[2] Mark 8:36

Another pointer to the fact of a singular source of joy can be gleaned from that revolutionary statement of Jesus to "pay Caesar what belongs to Caesar – and God what belongs to God."[3] It has been a subject of much biblical debate, many understanding it as some call to a duplication of our lives in which we pay Caesar his due (whatever Caesar means in our individual lives) and pay God his own due. But indeed, as Eugene Boring argued, the fact is that both Caesar and the coin being paid to him belong to God who made all things, bright and beautiful, all creatures great and small. "God's kingdom embraces all, including that of Caesar."[4] Hence it is limiting to understand Jesus' instruction as an indication that contentment could arise from satisfying some life conditions while God is taken as just one of those conditions. No, God is the main condition for joy and contentment. All other factors revolve round him and are subject to him. Our different actions and choices are therefore only meaningful in as much as they defer to Him. While giving Caesar his due is necessary for administrative and life purposes, getting going and fulfilled in life calls us to beware of what "Caesar" is in our lives. To be joyful and fulfilled, all "Caesars" in our lives must be subject to God.

To see "paying God his due" and "satisfying Caesar" on the same par is to resort to that kind of futility which the rich man in the earlier parable found himself. It never brings the desired joy and fulfilment. God is the only source of joy and fulfilment, in whom we live, move and have our being. All other stuff: riches, material well-being, the "Caesars", name them, are only little instruments to be prudently used in accessing that singular source of joy.

---

3   Mark 12:17.
4   M. Eugene Boring, *Mark: A Commentary*, (Kentucky: Westminster John Knox Press, 2006), P. 336.

12

$\mathcal{F}$ire on $\mathcal{E}$arth

"When Christ calls a man, he bids him come and die."
Dietrich Bonhoeffer, *The Cost of Discipleship*

There is the joke about Martin, an enthusiastic Catholic who kept inviting his agnostic friend to the church for a long time without success. One particular Saturday the agnostic suddenly said he was coming along to church the next day, probably just to get Martin off his back. The joy of Martin is best left to imagination. He called his priest straight away to give the good news of the possibility of a new convert. Just before the end of the telephone conversation Martin asked, "By the way Father, what is the liturgy about tomorrow?" The priest goes, "about Jesus saying I have come to bring fire on earth and how I wish it was burning now!" Martin could not but hide his uneasiness and reluctantly asked "but Father must we read that tomorrow?"

One can appreciate the apprehension of Martin. The impression of the startling statements of Jesus about "bringing fire to the earth" and "causing division between households" [1] creates some concern even for a strong faithful. Apparently other passages like "Jesus raises the widow's only son from the dead", or "Jesus eats and welcomes sinners", or "Jesus says come to me all that are overburdened and I will give you rest" would have been more inviting, more presentable images of the Lord. But as we well know, the words of the scriptures are not mere prose but deep messages which call for a special understanding.

Take some time to think about the reality of change in our lives. Think about those times when meaningful change has to be made either by yourself or by some other person. Changes, ordinarily, do not come easy, they bring some challenges. Indeed as Louis L'amour says, "each of us in his own ways wars against change."[2] Changes challenge our status quo, jolting us to the pain of adjustment. Yet the import of the gospel is a call to change. If the gospel which Jesus came to preach canvasses for realities like justice, like getting rid of evil, like challenging us to a stop of some vice or the other, then naturally there would be some fire at work. The Christian message by default calls for a standing-up for some value. In our world there are a lot of confusion and grey areas, for instance in the field of morality. With this sort of statement like "I have come to bring division", Jesus already alerts us of the painful decisions that would have to be made when such grey areas are confronted in life. To say "I believe" as we usually do in the Creed is to sign up for a set of values; it is to say "I choose this as against that".

We do not need to look far to see the practical consequences of this statement of Jesus in the lives of those who profess faith in him. We see this lived out in the heroic experiences of people like Thomas More who refused to reject his faith even at the threat of death; Maximilian Kolbe who witnessed to the cause of faith even unto death; Oscar Romero of El Salvador who died because he stood

---

[1]   Luke 12:49-53.
[2]   Louis L'amour, *The Lonely Men*, (New York: Bantam Books, 1984), p. 194.

for justice. But we also see the practical wisdom of Jesus' affirmation in the lives of less popular but countless millions who continually go through some denial, humiliation, rejection, pain and sometimes death daily on account of their beliefs and values. A number of times we too have lived out this experiences, maybe not to the point of death, but surely with the scars of pain, victimization, discrimination, some sacrifice, all because of some article of faith we profess in Jesus or which we hold about his Church. Faith in Christ does bring a consequence. To stand for values as great as those that Christ preached could not but bring its often not-too-sweet consequences.

The point is that this fiery statement of Jesus does not portray a violent part of him, as one would naturally want to think. Rather, it in fact complements what we have always known of him as the prince of peace.[3] For true peace is not the absence of war (or states of unpleasantness), but the presence of justice. And justice and its accolades do not come without some price. There is a life to which Christ calls man. It is a life in which a grain of wheat dies to produce many, whereas if it does not die it remains one. The plenitude of life which Jesus brings to his followers is achieved in a daily "dying" in struggles for truth, justice, right and the good. That is the fire he desired; those are the divisive struggles he spoke of.

---

[3] Isaiah 9:6.

13

Pride

Nothing is more opposed to God than pride, for self-deification is concealed in it.

-St. Philaret of Moscow.

The popular saying is that pride goes before a fall. There is the joke about a minister who, walking down the street on a cool evening, saw a circle of boys, shouting and cheering. In the center of the circle, he saw a dog. Fearing for the dog's safety, the minister poked his nose into the circle. "What's going on here?" he demanded. The oldest said, "It's just a stray. We all want him, so we're having a contest to decide who gets him. Whoever tells the biggest lie wins." The minister was furious. "You should not be telling lies. Don't you know it's a sin to lie? When I was your age, I never told a lie once!" The boys all hung their heads in silence. The youngest gave a deep sigh and said, "Fine, give him the dog."

Pride is not necessarily a negative reality.[1] There is a sense in which we are proud and necessarily so. We are proud of our possibilities for instance, our ability to do this or do that. Some level of pride is present in each human, given the high dignity we have been accorded with in life. The problem is when this basic and natural pride oversteps its bound and seeks to take control. And it is wont to do this, as the little boys figured in the joke above.

Jesus' parable about the choice of seats when invited to a banquet is instructive. He suggested taking the lowest sit so that when called up higher one gets honoured. Whereas if a higher seat had been taken, one could be eventually asked to give it up for someone else. Now the man who takes a lower sit does not necessarily take a sit that corresponds to his capacity or rating or importance. He merely takes a sit that corresponds to his virtue of humility. Humility is a virtue which one can practice without fear. It is a bag of possibilities from which tons of goodies can be brought out; whereas pride limits our possibilities by the very fact of its haughty claims.

Sometimes it is difficult to notice the ugly signs of pride. Indeed not to be noticeable is itself part of the nature of pride and thus calls for a discerning attention on our part. While the more popular show of pride which we often encounter is explicit and clear, sometimes pride also reeks in the human character in covert ways. The haughty man who speaks of himself always, or the lady who disdains the other because of looks and possessions are figures of pride which are easy to recognize. But what about the inability to recognize our limits? Often that is not easily discernible yet it is a central form of pride. For while humility knows and acknowledges its strength and weaknesses, pride sprints where angels fear to tread. Pride lacks the simplicity of saying "this is beyond me; A or B is better at this." Hence this vice is often

---

[1] See Paul's use of pride for instance in Galatians 6:4. While the New International Version of the bible renders the Greek verb 'κα χημα' as "to pride", the new Jerusalem Bible renders it as 'to boast'.

described as an overblown opinion of one's capabilities, rendering one unable to see limitations for what they are: not flaws but reality.

A cursory look at the history of salvation also gives us an insight into how the virtue of humility has always been upheld almost as a sine qua non for walking with God. In the biblical figures of persons like Moses, Job and Mary we see the expression of the delight of God with humble persons. The *Magnificat* of Mary is a most important laud in honour of humility and a chronicle of God's rejection of pride.[2] Stories like the conquest of the powerful but arrogant Goliath by a wee shepherd boy are also meant to show the constant divine preference of the humble to the proud.

Considering the fact that pride is this limiting, cutting off a wealth of support that one could have when one's limitation is not acknowledged, prudence suggests that such a vice be dumped. There is an array of gifts and talents given to different persons, but nobody is an island. A tree is always in need of a lot more trees to make up a forest; and to form a whole, parts are always necessary. There is therefore some reciprocity which must be recognized and appreciated for life to become even more wonderful and for our strength and possibilities to flower into life.

---

[2]   See Luke 1:46-55.

14

Such a Love

He's gone and turned my crazy world back around, and I've been saved by love.

-Amy Grant

Anthropomorphism is a big word but which simply means the conception of God in human terms. It is the tendency to explain the mystery of the being of God using human parameters and understanding. And that is fine, because we cannot conceive anything outside of our being. But then our understanding of God is therefore often limited.

One of such ways in which anthropomorphism limits our horizon in thinking of God exhibits itself when we think of the parable of the lost sheep. It is incredulous that the shepherd could leave 99 sheep on the mountain in search of a lost one. He leaves 99 sheep in peril and in danger of a possible attack, in search of one that he does not even have an assurance of ever finding! Such is the daring attitude of the shepherd. But much important, such is the love he has for each of the sheep of his flock.

The wisdom of the parable would be lost on us if we do not focus on the main message of the parable: "there will be more rejoicing in heaven over one sinner repenting than over ninety-nine upright people who have no need of repentance."[1] The subject of the parable is the enduring love of God for each and every soul. He is not oblivious of the predicaments of each one of his creatures. Our sojourn in this journey of faith is such a priority in his heart that he walks with us individually. And the journey is never boring to him even though it appears like such to us. He is ever present; He is the omnipresent.

The story is recounted of the man who saw his lifetime flash by in a dream. At very good times of his life he noticed four footprints: those of himself and those of God walking by his side always. But at difficult times he was astonished to notice just two footprints! What could this be", he asked himself. "God is a deserter who leaves us at moments of needs?" The answer came just before he woke from his dream. God enlightened him, "Those two footprints you saw were not yours my dear. They were mine. For at those difficult times I was carrying you."

We continually relive in our individual lives this splendid love which in human terms would be described as wasteful. St. Augustine is argued today to be one of the most important Fathers of the Church, if not the most important, and certainly the most influential of the early Church Fathers. His popular life history is however instructive. In his early years Augustine lived a dissolute life, even though ever wandering in search of a true meaning in life, but often in futile ways. He referred to his conduct in those days as memories of "past wickedness and carnal corruption."[2] It is an admission of how he wandered far from the source of life, becoming to himself "a wasteland."[3] Today, Augustine is an icon of faith.

---

[1]   Luke 15:7
[2]   Augustine, *Confessions*, Book II, Chapter 1.
[3]   *Op. Cit.,* Book II, Chapter 10.

Much more importantly, he is an icon of the enduring love of God who is always willing and desirous that all wandering feet return to the path of life. And God is never tired of doing this. It is his nature to love; it is not an extraneous duty to him, nor is it an extra function. It belongs to his very nature to will our good and do so in a grossly generous manner.

The snag however, as always, lies with man, the recipient of this generous love. Man often finds himself in that temptation to think that he is forever lost, long-gone. Yet the Father keeps waiting by the door with his arms wide open in a loving embrace for all his children, such a waiting so intense and borne out of a flowing love that Timothy Keller is tempted to describe it in his book as prodigal.[4]

The parable of the lost sheep which recounts the search for a single sheep at the risk of losing ninety nine is a parable designed to communicate the enduring and generous love of the Father. He is a Father not sometimes, but always.

---

[4] See Timothy Keller, *The Prodigal God, Recovering the Heart of the Christian Faith*, (New York: Penguin Group, 2008).

15

$\mathcal{T}$he one $\mathcal{M}$ission for all

Some give to the missions by going; others go by giving
-Unknown

It must have been a really beautiful scene when Jesus proclaimed the reason for his coming amongst us. On that fateful day, He had gone into the synagogue in Nazareth his home town and proclaimed what we could call his mission statement. "The spirit of the Lord is on me", he said, "For he has anointed me to bring good news to the afflicted...."[1] And all eyes were upon him because there was recognition of some awe in the heart of all. There was something significantly different in this young man; there was an unquantifiable hope in his words.

Indeed that was the mission of Jesus, to bring hope to mankind and to show that salvation resides in Him alone, in that single name by which mankind is saved.[2] This mission which Jesus undertook

---

[1]   Luke 4: 16-22
[2]   Acts of Apostles 4:12

over two thousand years ago He eventually handed on to his trusted friends and apostles. Over successive years and through successive peoples, languages and cultures, that same mission has been preached, accomplishing the words of the psalmist "their message reaches the whole world."[3]

This mission remains the mission of all baptized, all to whom the Spirit of the Lord has been given to drink. For been baptized into his death, and been raised up with him at his resurrection, we have received the mandate to "go therefore, make disciples of all nations."[4] The mission therefore is just one, even though the mode in which each carries out that injunction might differ.

Each one of us, in our individual state of life, has the best of chances to carry out the mission of Christ, He who came that we may have life and have it abundantly. Thus, even though some are specially chosen, commissioned or ordained to carry out the propagation of this mission in some special way, the mission belongs to all. The Holy Father in his 2013 World Mission message declared that "the missionary tasks, that of broadening the boundaries of faith, belongs to all baptized persons."[5]

It is always amazing to think of the huge success which the mission has had. From the proverbial mustard seed it has grown to a huge salvation tree, spreading through the whole world. The success of the mission message in spite of upheavals which it has suffered over two millennia speaks volume. The painful persecution the Church has suffered and continues to suffer in contemporary days; the several scandals that rocked the Church of God; the many challenges that modernity poses to the gospel all come together to open our eyes to the assurance of Christ that no power of the underworld or whatsoever power could ever bring down this mission.

---

[3]   Psalm 19:4
[4]   Matthew 28:19
[5]   See Message of Pope Francis for World Mission Day, 2013, number 2.

As we reflect on the mission of Christ to all baptized, it is important to remember this mission is not accomplished only in actions but also through prayers. I have never stopped wondering why the Church named St. Therese of Lisieux the patroness of the missions alongside St. Francis Xavier. This humble woman never stepped out on missions to any territory. She spent most part of her very short religious life within the convent. She died at the very young age of twenty four. The desire of St. Therese for the missions was however evident. Even though she lived an unknown life, Therese recognized the universal mandate to us all to propagate the good news, constantly praying for missionaries. Her choice as patroness of missions is evidently a reminder to us of Paul's recognition of the fact that "I did the planting, Apollos did the watering, but God gave growth."[6] Therese's nearness to God in supplications for the missions is by itself an enormous lesson for us.

The mission of Christ continues to be the mission of us all. As at 2010 when the world population stood at 6.9 billion, just 32% of that figure professed Christianity.[7] Hence, immense as the success of proclaiming the saving message of Christ has been, even much more is yet to be done. This shall be achieved in the generous use of our resources and talents. In our simple testimony of faith to all and sundry, in our constant prayers for missions and missionaries, the message of the gospel shall continue to sound abroad. That mission remains very much entrusted to you and me.

---

[6]   1 Corinthians 3:6

[7]   See The Pew Forum on Religion and Public Life, "Global Christianity – A Report on the Size and Distribution of the World's Christian Population", December 2011.

16

Thanksgiving

Gratitude is not only the greatest of virtues, but the parent
of all others

> \- Cicero

An ingrate is a colleague of a robber, goes the saying. Giving thanks is
therefore not just some political correctness in etiquette but a human
virtue. It is interesting to note that the greatest prayer of the Christian,
the Eucharistic sacrifice, takes its name from "giving thanks", the
thanksgiving of the most worthy of all men and at once our God, Jesus,
to the Father on our behalf. It is a thanksgiving which becomes our
own thanksgiving to the Father of all good.

The time of thanksgiving is a time to look back to the array of
goodness with which we have been blessed. It is a time to cast our minds
back and sing of the goodness of the Lord, counting our blessings and
showing gratitude. It is a time to be attentive to the small things of life
which have made our lives meaningful but which are often taken for

granted. In his new poem *The Hosanna of Small Mercies*, John Agard beautifully recounted the blink of the green leaf, the smell of coffee, the musk from old books on the shelves as the part of those little blessings we often neglect in life.[1]

The question therefore comes home to us: what are those gifts in life that we often take for granted? What are those small mercies in our lives which often do not occur to us particularly as being gifts worthy of continuous gratitude? Why not let us start first with my life, your life, our lives! There is a common experience I have had with old Italians. Whenever I ask one of them, usually a grandma or grandpa, "how are you feeling today?", the response is almost prototype, "thank God, Father. As long as I wake up and put my feet on the ground I am grateful." It has become such a pattern of response that it has made me to see a fundamental value of gratitude underlying such a response. Yet often we wake up full of energy and just bounce away, taking it for granted that another day has merely begun, *nothing much*! Oh no, it is something very much for that old man or woman who also used to bounce and run, but now is slowed down by age, yet recognizes the immense gift of life and gives thanks for that. Perhaps there is some wisdom that comes from aging. We can learn from that wisdom and gain wisdom of heart. We are a project of wonder and every moment of our existence calls for an experience of sentiments of thanksgiving to God for the wonder of our being.

Another reason for thanksgiving but which often is shrouded in some *forgotteness* is our family. What a gift often taken for granted. Because we are together most of the time, surrounded by each other, we forget the uniqueness and joy we represent to each other in the family. Sometimes the frictions of daily existence even make this *forgotteness* more acute. There is none that feels the need to be grateful to his family members than the immigrant, far away from home, often not

---

[1]   This beautiful piece in fact won the Queen's gold medal for poetry in 2012.

because he wants to be far but because of the exigencies of livelihood. He lives daily the pain of not been surrounded by the family, that family which ordinarily is taken for granted! So give thanks for your children, your wife, and your husband. A constant pat on the back, a grateful hug, a kiss of appreciation, are all wise little acts to recognize the wealth of these small mercies.

The gift of little things in life: laughter, smile, company. These are gifts to be remembered when we ponder on thanksgiving. A verse of the song *thank you for giving me the morning* says "thank you I have my occupation, thank you for every pleasure small; thank you for music, light and gladness thank you for them all!" Nothing best solidifies the truth of those words than the experience of a friend of mine who was caught in the power outage of Toronto on July 8, 2013 after an extreme thunderstorm. According to him, this experience "was like a momentary death." Since they were hardly ever needed, not having candles or flashlights in the house sent him into a state of panic and helplessness.[2] Of course I told him he needed to take a lesson from St. Francis of Assisi who had great love for and paid much attention to all of nature's gifts, including light! Let there be thanksgiving for little things therefore: for light, music, gladness.

All good things come from the Father of mercies. In the final analysis, after being grateful to all creatures, to God belongs the sum of our thanksgiving for all good things come from him.[3] Let there be thanksgiving always in all hearts.

---

[2]   Even though I told him this was a common experience in an average developing city. A child in my village in Nigeria would actually suspect a problem if there was no power outage in a day!

[3]   Beautifully expressed in the wise lyrics of that song "All things bright and beautiful, all creatures great and small; all things wise and wonderful, the Lord God made them all."

17

Divine Mercy

He saved us, not because of righteous things we had done,
but because of his mercy

-Titus 3:5, NIV.

The canonization of the Polish nun Mary Faustina Kowalska on April 30, 2000 was one of the canonizations done by John Paul II in his last days in office. It came approximately five years before his death. But it was a most important function for the Holy Father. Not only because it was yet another fruit of devotion and sign of the growth of the faith in his native land, but essentially because the divine mercy experience which Faustina received came as a big relief at a most tumultuous time in the lives of both the Saint and the Pontiff. Faustina had had her experience of the mercy of the Lord over the period of the two world wars, a time which was particularly difficult for the Holy Father himself considering the horrors Poland went through. At that time of great pain and sorrow all over the world, the Lord revealed to Faustina that "humanity will not find peace until it turns trustfully to divine mercy."[1] The placing of the feast of Divine Mercy on the second Sunday of Easter was therefore not inadvertent. It was purposeful, to show the fact of the mercy of God shown to humanity in the suffering, death and resurrection of the Son of God. It was meant to instruct us of the salvation won by Christ and shown to us in those blessed two rays of mercy revealed to Faustina, two rays which, as Jesus had explained to her, represent the blood and water flowing from his saving side.

This message of the immense mercy which Christ bestowed on all of humanity is a message that calls the attention of all Christians to what matters in our Christian calling: we have all been saved by mercy. This same mercy is awaited by millions of people "who, afflicted by a particularly harsh trial or crushed by the weight of the sins they committed, have lost all confidence in life and are tempted to give in to despair"[2] Humanity suffers a great deal. The body of Christ, dispersed in all places in the lives of millions of people, continues to relive pains and sorrows. The hallmark of the divine mercy message is a call to action to ameliorate these sufferings and pains. And there is an immense lot which can be achieved by us in doing same. Pains and hurts do not fall from space in some mysterious ways. Often they are direct actions of man to man, or consequences of the same. The divine mercy Himself tastes of this pain and through his message to Sister Faustina beckons on all called by His name to make amends, to restore smiles and to alleviate pains.

The Christian message becomes suspect if it shuns the important necessity of healing pains and showing the mercy of God at work. The essential character of the gospel is the unconditional mercy and love of God. A love shown in almost a "wasteful" manner; a love shown to the symbolic prodigal son who had wasted his patrimony abroad, in a land

---

[1]   *Diary of St. Faustina*, p. 132
[2]   Homily of John Paul II on the canonization of Sr. Mary Faustina Kowalska, 30 April, 2000.

of sin; a love shown to Peter who would eventually deny the master yet was the one made the foundation of the Church; a love given to the thief on the Cross; a lavish display of love and mercy.

The divine mercy as a feast and reality calls us to an understanding of the constant state of action in which we must be found, pouring the oil of relief on the wounds of humanity. That man who fell into the hands of brigands found mercy in the merciful attention of the Samaritan. It is indicative of the fact that there is always a choice. There is a choice of passing by while several around suffer. There is a choice of looking on, aloof, while our brothers and sisters pass through a difficult situation. It is easy to comfort oneself with statements like "it is not my business" or "I mind my business." But the words of Faustina are applicable to each and every Christian or else such a person is not a Christian. The apostle of mercy says "I feel tremendous pain when I see the sufferings of my neighbours. All my neighbours' sufferings reverberate in my own heart; I carry their anguish in my heart in such a way that it even physically destroys me. I would like all their sorrows to fall upon me, in order to relieve my neighbour."[3] Those are awesome words and seem only pertinent to a saint. Not quite so. They are as a matter of fact applicable to every baptized who should grow to be like the Master[4], he who came to save and give life abundantly.

So who needs mercy around you? Do you see anyone in a state of despair, agitation, hunger, fear, error or helplessness? Yes, that is the body of Jesus that awaits your mercy. For "in truth I tell you, in so far as you did this to one of the least of these brothers of mine, you did it to me."[5]

---

[3]   *Diary of St. Faustina*, p. 365.
[4]   Matthew 10:25
[5]   Matthew 25:40

That other Side of Glory

> In the course of our lives, the evil which in itself we seek most to shun, and which, when we are fallen into, is the most dreadful to us, is oftentimes the very means or door of our deliverance - Daniel Defoe in *Robinson Crusoe*

The apostles of Christ are often referred to as the "glorious twelve" because of their heroic contribution to the spread of faith and the martyrdom that all of them except John suffered, going by Sacred Tradition. The title "glorious" is not misplaced. These were individuals who submitted themselves to be used as tools for the greater glory of God. They were nonetheless human beings.

The humanity of the apostles showed itself in several instances in the scriptures. One of such instances was on the Mount Tabor, the mount of transfiguration, where they had seen the glory of Jesus in all its fullness and power, attested by the presence of Moses and Elijah, symbols of the law and the prophets respectively. The immediate response of the three apostles as voiced by Peter, the more impetuous, was "Lord, it is wonderful for us to be here; if you want me to, I will make three shelters here, one for you, one for Moses and one for Elijah."[1] That was the reasoning and the voice of man. Man naturally seeks the condition that promotes his physical well-being, any condition that leans towards a perceived good, serenity or pleasure.

Jesus however had a shocker in the cooler for Peter, a shocker that would also be applicable to all the apostles and all of us to whom they have eventually communicated the message of salvation. The shocker is precisely the message that peace, good, serenity, pleasure, glory and all these desirable conditions of well-being are not *stand-alones*. They are not conditions that are achievable solely by themselves. They always come with some sacrifice. They are products of a dialectic.

For the apostles who saw the dazzling glory and serene beauty, it was desirable to stay up there and conserve the moment, never letting it go. Jesus however had a great lesson for them. The beauty and glory which they saw could not possibly be conserved without the will of the Father being fulfilled. The will of the Father was for Jesus to purify humanity by his passion. "The Son of Man is destined to suffer grievously", he told them.[2] They must therefore leave that mountain of glory and return to the plains of ordinary life, where the scriptures would eventually be fulfilled.

The question of the cross in life situations is never quite palatable. But it is also inevitable. Though the state of glory on the mountain was desirable, Jesus meant to show his disciples the position of the cross in Christian life. The crown of thorns which he bore was a cruel symbol of the real crown he was to wear as the King of Kings, conqueror of death and the grave. Moments of the cross often leave us

---

[1]   Matthew 17:4.

[2]   Luke 9:22.

deluded and confused. We wish it never came and sometimes its pain even leads us to do or say things which are almost on the verge of blasphemy. We raise several questions and put the goodness of God to doubt.

The experience of the three apostles on mount Tabor should serve us as a magnifying glass in seeing better the complete picture of life. Great glory comes with great sacrifices; the cross is not an opposite of glory but just another side to a complete perception of glory. Difficult moments of our lives must be seen in brighter lights.

The experience of Jesus is equally instructive to us with regards to our perception of glory and difficulties. He was transfigured all right on that mountain, he was glorified. But he was also aware of the coming trying times. With resolute will he embraced these seemingly contrasting experiences, constantly reminding the apostles of the fate that awaited him in Jerusalem. Jesus' acceptance of a difficult time did not make him oblivious to the past time of serenity and grace. The ability to make that distinction is quite helpful. When troubles and sufferings arise, it is a Christian obligation not to fall into the temptation of seeing only the present shadows, while ignoring the splendour of the past and the silver linings of the future.

Passing through trying times, no matter what we define "trying" to be, is complementary to our holistic growth. It is but the other side of a glory we have already known or is yet to come.

19

$\mathcal{T}$reasures in $\mathcal{E}$arthenware

God does not call the perfect, he perfects those he calls.

-Unknown

The story of John Mary Vianney is one that would always be cherished in the history of the Church. It is a story which underscores the frailty of humanity. It also shows the fact that fruitfulness as a Christian is not so much a product of individual efforts as it is the workings of God in us. If individual efforts are useful and necessary, they are such in as much as they are open to the fructifying grace of divinity. John Mary Vianney was an average student and had difficulties with his studies. "He struggled poorly in his courses but succeeded in being ordained a priest in August 13, 1815."[1] But after his ordination, working in the remote village of Ars, this simple man of God was such a formidable instrument of evangelization, particularly in confessions, that his

---

[1]   Rosemary Ellen Guiley, *The Encyclopedia of* Saints, s.v. "John Baptist Mary Vianney", (New York: Visionary Living Inc.), p. 175.

fame spread abroad. The man who had been taunted by his peers as uneducated enough to be a Parish Priest had as much as 300 visitors and converts streaming to the village of Ars daily to have his wise counsel at the confessional.

St. Paul understood the nature of the mystery of God, with regards to His choice of human instruments in salvation history. He would often refer to himself with terms like unworthy, "the least of the apostles"[2], "greatest of sinners."[3] Of course the fact that a man who once persecuted the Church of God to death eventually changed to a preacher of the good news was enough to show Paul how indeed unworthy he was. It is the same wisdom which is taught in the theology of the ministries. The priest acts *in persona Christi*, meaning he acts in the name of Christ who alone is the Priest. All other priests participate in the fullness of His priesthood. The grace and anointing with which the priest is bequeathed therefore flows from the only one source, the Vine, without whom nothing good can be done.[4] The priest's actions are effective therefore not because of his worthiness but because they flow from the power of Christ who acts through and within the sacraments.

The sense of dependence and unworthiness analyzed above does not pertain only to the ministries or the ordained. Rather it reminds us that each and every Christian is fruitful in Christ and in Him alone. The experience of Peter and the other apostles after Jesus' resurrection comes handy here[5]. After a fruitless night of fishing, the risen Lord appeared to Peter and asked him to cast the net to the starboard. That was exactly what they were doing all night! But as soon as Peter threw the net out, just as the Lord commanded, "they could not haul it in because of the quantity of fish."[6] It was enough an experience for

---

[2] 1 Corinthians 15:9.
[3] 1 Timothy 1:15.
[4] John 15:5
[5] See John 21:1-6.
[6] John 21:6.

the beloved disciple to realize "it is the Lord."[7] Of course, it is the Lord of fruitfulness. That same net that had seemed impossible; that same throw onto the starboard that had proved futile all night; that same hope of catching some fish. But some difference here: there is the coming onto the scene of the Lord who brings all aspirations to completion. That is what makes the difference. It was all the difference ever needed: the jewel that makes the earthenware precious.

Since the omnipotence of God is not questionable, the concern for the competence of the human instruments he uses is not so much the issue. The greater issue is the configuration of these human instruments to him. Jesus invites all baptized to a life of union with him, a life in which true meaning is gained. Our availability and readiness is therefore what matters as such. Competence comes thereafter. In the journey of faith, God himself is the main actor, inviting us onto the turf of loyalty and trust. It is only with this realization that the initiative to save and to make fruitful comes from him that we can truly be successful and confidently walk with He who writes on crooked lines.

---

[7]   John 21:7.

20

I believe in the Resurrection of the Dead

If there is no resurrection of the dead, then Christ cannot have been raised either

1 Corinthians 15:13

My Bishop has a very catchy joke about going to heaven. Once in a while in his homilies he would ask "how many want to go to heaven?" Of course all the hands in the congregation are up and flailing. But then he asks the next question, "Who wants to go now?" Gradually the hands begin to go down one by one! Not many are ready to go immediately of course.

The belief in the resurrection of the dead is one of the cardinal hinges of our faith. It is an important belief which sums up the reason for our hope and the future of our faith. By baptism, we are not only baptized into the death of Christ but also raised to life by his resurrection. The ultimate focus of the Christian is therefore a gaze on that future life with the Trinity, a life which never ends and which would never experience corruption.

The time of death of our loved ones does bring us sorrow and pain. It is understandable if, because we are human, we experience in a most radical way the agony of living without those who were so dear to us. We experience within us the agony of letting go and the pains of never seeing again in the flesh those whom we have always loved. Even Jesus, though he would eventually raise Lazarus up, shed tears at the news of his death. It is one of the few instances in which the humanity of Jesus is so aptly depicted in the scriptures. Grieving for the loss of a loved one is therefore part of our humanity.

Much as our emotions take over when death occurs, the conviction of our faith must never be thrown into oblivion. For the wealth of the scriptures teaches us how deceptive the pains of the present could be. The sting of death could at times be so disillusioning as to paint before us a picture of despair. At the passing of our loved ones, it appears as if all is ended. Yet the sum of our life is just seventy, or eighty for those who are strong.[1] No matter the age of these departed loved ones, young or old, they cannot outlive an infinitesimally insignifi cant dot of eternity which God has prepared for those who love him. It is in the world which never ends that real life begins. The present seventy or eighty is but a faint prelude to a life that knows neither cessation nor end.

If the present life is just a temporary passage to the real life, and if we are on a journey to what St. Paul calls our "homeland", it is not only desirable in the light of faith but also in the perception of logic that we should make the necessary efforts and sacrifice to secure such a glorious life. There is no forfeiture which could outweigh the value of eternal bliss. The joy of the resurrection and the hope of eternity with God is such a pivotal part of our faith that St. Paul rightly pointed

---

[1]   Psalm 90:10

out that "if our hope in Christ has been for this life only, we are of all people, the most pitiable."[2] The permanent reality of heaven is the consolation which keeps the light of faith ablaze in us, in spite of the adversities, setbacks, disappointments and even death.

Life is beautiful indeed, as we have all experienced at different points of our existence. It is so beautiful that sometimes we may want to take the passing away of loved ones as a mere resignation to fate rather than an active acceptance of a desirable reality. A Yoruba adage says "the savour of meat in the mouth is so good that if we had the opportunity we would want to continue eating it without ever swallowing it"[3] But we really cannot. Sometimes, we merely accept the necessity of death in form of an unwilling resignation like that captured in the adage above. But the reality of dying cannot just be merely passively accepted. It is a reality of the moment of glory. For the essence of creation, as the Baltimore Catechism simply teaches: is to know God, love Him and to serve Him in this world. All of these in order to be happy with Him forever in heaven.

If that last phrase "to be happy with Him for ever in heaven" is therefore not true or in some way unrealizable, or if faith in the resurrection of the dead is at long last found to be a myth, we would indeed be "a people most pitiable." But as Blaise Pascal's wager does remind us, even if when we die we realize there is no reality like heaven or even God, we would not have lost much. If however we eventually discover that there is indeed heaven when we die, not believing in such a reality would have cost us such an irreparable lot. A rational person would therefore want to make the choice of believing and working towards this reality. The difference here is that our faith is more than a guess work. It is the power of faith at work in us: a guarantee of blessings we hope for; a proof of the existence of realities we are yet to see.[4]

---

2   1 Corinthians 15:19

3   The Yoruba people in the South West of Nigeria would say "Ó wu ni ká jeran pé lénu, ònfà òfun ni ò jé."

4   Hebrews 11:1

21

Seeing with Inner Eyes

The Spirit explores the depths of everything, even the depths of God.

1 Corinthians 3:10

It is a fortunate thing to be educated. There is a whole world of horizon that one gains in going to school and learning. The society is also better for it, since the more educated its citizens are the more functional such a society becomes. But it is one thing to go to school and be educated; it is another thing to actually learn and grow from such a knowledge acquired. There is a form of learning which is a mere fulfilment of the requirements of academics while true learning empowers, making one perceive reality in a special manner. Education, truly appropriated, is a clear magnifying lens with which we see things more clearly.

In the experience of Jesus asking his apostles "who do people say I am"[1], he shows us the importance of "being educated" but at once

---

[1]   Matthew 16:13

he makes us realize mere education is not the deal. It is merely the condition necessary to open up the student to learning and perceiving of reality in a most special way. The apostles had been schooled under the tutelage of Jesus when he asked them this question in Caesarea Philippi. Going by the three synoptic gospel accounts of this episode, the apostles had spent quite some time with Jesus who was now advance in his public ministry. In response to Jesus' question as to who the people said he was, the apostles recounted the several opinions of the people: John the Baptist, Elijah, one of the prophets. It however took the illumination of the inner sight for Peter to acclaim Jesus for who he was, "You are the Christ, the Son of the living God."[2] Jesus of course made him realize this was no knowledge from the ordinary, it came from an inner illumination. For "it was no human agency that revealed this to you but my Father in heaven."[3] Thus even though Peter, together with the other apostles had been schooled in the life of faith and had learnt at length from Jesus, there was yet the need for an inner sight, an illumination for him to perceive the reality of the person of Jesus for what it really was. Mere education was not enough.

It takes the inner eyes to see some reality clearly. Not everything is available to the naked eye. The working of the Holy Spirit which enlightens us is more often than not hidden from the ordinary human sight and reasoning. Take for instance the immediate episode after Peter confessed Jesus as Lord at Caesarea Philippi. Jesus revealed his true mission to the apostles for the first time, making it clear that "he was destined to go to Jerusalem and suffer grievously at the hands of the elders and chief priests and scribes."[4] The same Peter who had been enlightened by the Holy Spirit and had rightly proclaimed Jesus as Christ from an inner sight spontaneously declared "this must not

---

[2]   Matthew 16:16
[3]   Matthew 16:17
[4]   Matthew 16:21

happen to you."[5] Peter could not in any way conceive that the "Christ", the Messiah or the anointed one, could suffer. It was contradictory to the senses. The Messiah saves, he does not suffer. And so Peter spontaneously, in his human fervour, rejects such a proposition for Jesus. He refused to see from the inner sight. He focused on reality squarely from the outside. The knowledge which he had been given by inner sight is contradictory to that which he experiences in the outward, ordinary school of life.

In our lives too there are a lot of things that appear meaningless, particularly when our faith dictates some course of action which is different from the natural way of acting. There are several conventional ways of behaviour or manner of seeing things which our faith chides us to leave behind or go against. But looking at these challenges from a purely human perspective often leaves us confused and out of tune with the more profound plan of the Spirit. The Christian, in order to make the best of the plans of the divine for his life, cannot afford to rest squarely on the outside looks. The rule of faith challenges us to several actions that are otherwise deemed ridiculous without the scrutiny of the inner eyes. For instance, giving out in alms, even though we are not swimming in plenty, is not a thing we are wont to do ordinarily. It takes the inner eye to see the example of the widow of Zarephath to remember that God works in wonders to fulfil his promises to those who love him.[6] In the same wise, making a drastic change of our lifestyle and promising to pay back those cheated in four-fold is not an experience that comes without some inner illumination. That was exactly what Zacchaeus did, having been instructed by such a joy that ruled from within.[7]

It takes the inner sight provided by the illumination of the Holy Spirit for us to see clearly, love dearly and follow nearly. The life of

---

[5]   Matthew 16:23
[6]   1 Kings 17:7-16.
[7]   Luke 19:1-10.

the Christian is a life essentially dependent on the new sight that the Spirit gives. And no Christian can afford to live only by the senses or merely by external perceptions. For we live by faith and not just by sight.

22

The Beauty of the Different

At bottom every man knows well enough that he is a unique being, only once on this earth; and by no extraordinary chance will such a marvellously picturesque piece of diversity in unity as he is, ever be put together a second time.
-Fredrick Nietzsche

Have you ever wondered what the world would be like if there was no diversity? Have you ever imagined peoples looking exactly the same, having the same choices of food, same type of professions, same choices of recreational activities and so on? Life, to say the least, would be endlessly boring. That in fact is an understatement. Boredom would be a euphemism for mediocrity or imperfection. The American Ecotheolgian Thomas Berry eloquently expresses this sentiment. "Diversity is the magic. It is the first manifestation, the first beginning of the differentiation of a thing and of simple identity. The greater the diversity, the greater the perfection."[1] There is an interesting pattern that emerges from differences and diversity which adds a most unique spice to life.

Interesting and desirable as diversity is however, often and again it meets with opposition. There seems to be some natural fear of the other, or at least prejudice against the one perceived to be *an other*. These are experiences that are natural to creatures, humans and animals alike. In the canine world for instance, there is a level of curiosity which the appearance of a Poodle arouses in a Yorkshire Terrier. The curiosity, if not abated by the owner of the terrier or by some other means, could escalate into a bark of protest and a possibility of an attack. Perhaps this is a tactic to maintain territory control or to show some superiority? In any case such a reaction to diversity is not limited to the lower animal. It is very prominent even among humans, and among humans who profess their belief in Christ. It does appear class-inclusion is a condition for the acceptance of the other. When such an inclusion is breached, diversity is perceived as a difference and interpreted as non- benign.

Indications from the scriptures lend support to the last affirmation. Take for instance one of the behaviours exhibited by the apostles of Christ. They had seen an individual casting out devils in the name of Jesus and wanted to stop them, for no other reason other than the fact that "he was not one of us."[2] Jesus used the opportunity to teach the apostles a lesson on inclusivity and on the importance of striving after a goal from a multidimensional approach. The diversity of the individual was not the issue to hold on to, but the nature and quality of what this different individual was doing. He was carrying out an essential aspect of the desires of Jesus who had come to liberate and set free and

---

[1]   See http://www.betterworld.net/heroes/pages-b/berry-quotes.htm
[2]   Mark 9:38

so posed no threat. Indeed, Jesus reminded them "anyone who is not against us is for us."[3]

It is true that diversity highlights the differences amongst people and sometimes reveals dissimilar way of doing things. But these dissimilar ways are not necessarily discrepant ways. The fact that I cook my veggies a bit while you eat it raw does not make us eaters of different veggies. We only eat it differently.

Simple as this analogy is, it is fundamental to the understanding of the diversity and yet richness which inheres amongst peoples. A heavy investment has been made by God in our persons. This investment is however as varied as it is heavy. The ability to harness together the variety of this investment would go a long way to determine the returns such an investment yields in us eventually. Seeing diversity as a blessing opens up an array of possibilities which the individual person with his natural limitations could not normally achieve.

Recognition and acceptance of diversity is an important virtue for the human person. For the Christian, it is more than a virtue. It is a necessity. The whole essence of Christianity is rubbished if the unity of creation and the beautiful interdependence of creatures are not upheld. St. Paul succinctly sums it up in his fine homage to variety and unity. "There are many different gifts, but it is always the same Spirit; there are many different way of serving, but it is always the same Lord. There are many different forms of activity, but in everybody it is the same God who is at work in them all."[4]

---

[3]   Mark 9:40

[4]   1 Corinthians 12:4-6

23

Love

There is no surprise more magical than the surprise of being
loved. It is God's finger on man's shoulder.

-Charles Morgan

There is the story about two monks who were on a quick errand to the
village next to their monastery. Usually they cross the river on their way
without a problem. This particular day however the river had overflown
its banks. But not only that. There was a young lady by the bank of
the river, helpless and not knowing how to cross over. The first of the
monks saw this lady in her helplessness, gave a courteous smile and
passed on. The other monk saw the lady, pondered a bit and offered to
carry her in his arms over the river. The young lady of course was full
of gratitude and both parties continued their journeys to their different
destination.

On the way back the first monk asked, "I cannot believe you
actually carried that lady over the river. You know we should keep a

respectable distance from ladies, especially young ladies!" The second monk looked at him and replied gently, "Brother, I dropped that lady by the riverbank this morning. It appears you are still carrying her weight."

There is no gainsaying the first monk wanted to be careful to observe the requisite laws and etiquette of their calling. But such a religious law which he was trying to keep actually has as its fulfilment the very sum of all laws: love. It is that same sum which the second monk has kept in this particular instance, and in doing so has fulfilled all laws. This instance also reveals how difficult putting love into practice could be under some life circumstances.

The word love is reputed to be one of the most used words in the human vocabulary. This statistics by itself underscores the primacy of love in life. The question is: how is the primacy of love and the much talk about love lived out in practical terms? Jesus had several discussions on the theme of love with his contemporaries, particularly the Pharisees. These disciplined people pride themselves on several counts and on good grounds too. They would clean the outside of dishes, strictly keep the Sabbath day and observe all religious laws to the letter. Jesus however pointed out that these laws were meant to be kept without losing track of their ultimate focus: the good and sanctification of man.

Thus Jesus, referring to such religious laws, would say "these you should have practiced, those not neglected."[1] By "those" Jesus was making reference to what he called "weightier matters of the Law – justice, mercy, good faith."[2] Thus the precepts of the law, whether religious or social (but particularly the religious) would always be pointers to a greater virtue: love; a love that bears fruit in the acts of justice, goodness, mercy, kindness etc.

It is interesting that several religions have made tremendous efforts towards living out the ideals of their beliefs in God. These ideals have

---

[1]   Matthew 23:23
[2]   *Ibid.*

been preserved from ages to ages and have become the guides for worshiping God under different religious creeds. The Jewish religion for instance prides itself of having received 613 commandments from Yahweh God, of which 365 are prohibitions, and 248 precepts. With such hundreds of laws, it is best left to imagination the intricate moral decisions that would have to be undertaken at several times in order to discern what was licit to do. And this is just for one religion.

However Jesus already pointed out that these myriads of laws should not cause us so much trouble. In response to the question of that teacher of the law as to the most important of all commandments, Jesus had replied it was love of God, followed by love of neighbour. Thus all the commandments, in spite of their classifications into hundreds as in the Jewish laws, are summed up in the precept of love.

No law could be claimed to have been kept if love is amiss; no good can be said to have been done in the absence of love. St. Paul paints the point in a very big canvass of imaginative words "though I command languages both human and angelic – if I speak without love, I am no more than a gong booming or a cymbal clashing."[3] The entire chapter of this letter of St. Paul which is popularly called a hymn to love further supports the same fact.

Indeed "in the evening of our lives", says St. John of the Cross, "we shall be judged on love."[4] A Love which is neither a product of individual whims and caprices nor a spinning infatuation which burns wildly today and wanes tomorrow. We are talking about love which is a deliberate act of will and a product of a conscious choice, sometimes unpleasurable. It is a love whose price cannot be paid since it is a "given" not a "merited".

Love is the sum of all laws.

---

[3]   1 Corinthians 13: 1ff.

[4]   St. John of the Cross, *Dichos* 64.

Christ our King

...And his reign will have no end.

-Luke 1:33

The closing hours of the earthly life of Jesus was filled with interesting episodes. One of such episodes is the long interrogation session Pilate had with him. The gospel of John particularly gives a detailed account of this encounter between Jesus and Pilate. One of Pilate's questions was if Jesus was a King. And Jesus answered that question in the positive, affirming that he was a King and was indeed "born for this, I came into the world for this."[1] In the feast of Christ the King, Christians celebrate the kingship of Jesus in the Church's liturgy. But more importantly, we recognize and worship Jesus' royalty in our lives. He is a king of all times, reigning over the entire universe.

The Catechism of the Church teaches us that by the virtue of our baptism, we share in the three offices of Jesus Christ: we share in his

---

[1] John 18: 33-37.

priestly, prophetic and kingly offices.[2] The knowledge that we share in the royalty of Jesus is surely thrilling, and necessarily so. It is an indication that we are special beings, a chosen nation having for itself a formidable leader. But the kingship of Jesus spells out an entirely different meaning of what it means to be a King or to reign over all peoples. Because his kingdom "is not of this world", a point he had made clear to Pilate, Jesus manifested to the apostles and to all of us who believe in him a radical understanding of royalty and its intricate connection with service.

In the parable of the multiplication of loaves, he taught us that his kingship is that of a leader who cares about the well-being of his subjects and would do all in his power to ensure same. In his washing of the feet of the apostles, he taught us that his kingship is not that of usurpation or of lording it over, but that of humble service. Even in a moment of pain like at the garden of Gethsemane, Jesus gave us a witness as to the sort of king that he was. In asking Peter not to fight and to sheath his sword, he taught that his kingship was not built on violence, nor sustained by one who is violent. Indeed he would later tell Pilate, "Mine is not a kingdom of this world; if my kingdom were of this world, my men would have fought to prevent my being surrendered to the Jews."[3] Finally in giving up willingly to death, even though in an unquantifiable agony, he taught us his kingship is that of a royal who gives up all, even his life, to save the subject.

This sort of royalty just literally blows you away. You will be right to say it is "out of this world." But again, all of the life of Jesus is a mine of gold from which Christians are called to draw. What he teaches us about his kingship is therefore a challenge to our conception of the royal, the powerful, and the mighty. Jesus is a sort of king who stoops to conquer. His kingship has a lot to teach us about positions of authority and leadership.

---

2   *Catechism of the Catholic Church*, 871.
3   John 18:37

No wonder we are awesomely attracted by this strong personality: a royalty born in a manger; a creator of all who pays taxes to fulfil order; a most powerful warrior who would not win by violence; a creator of all who stands at the door, knocking in the hope that someone would open his heart.

In a world that has lost a significant part of the meaning of what it means to lead and to be truly great, the kingship of Jesus again illumines our mind. The simple yet fascinating nature of his royalty calls us to an imitation of the true meaning of greatness. The great King himself recommends it. "Learn from me, for I am and gentle and humble in heart."[4]

---

4   Matthew 11:29

The Family: The Church at its Beginnings

> The family is, so to speak, the domestic church. In it parents should, by their word and example, be the first preachers of the faith to their children; they should encourage them in the vocation which is proper to each of them, fostering with special care vocation to a sacred state.
>
> -Lumen Gentium, 11.

The saying is that "a whole is the summation of its parts", and the strength of that whole depends on the strength of each individual part. This is so true of the Church of God. The Vatican II Council Fathers recognized this fact and referred to the family as the "domestic church". It is that unit without which the Church in its wholeness cannot quite function. The family unit is that mustard seed which, planted and nurtured well, produces a blooming and healthy Church.

John Paul II particularly developed this vision of the Council in his detailed attention to the nature and beauty of the Christian family. His understanding of the family as a participation in the salvific ministry of Christ is enlightening. Through this ministry, the human society is built up. "Christian marriage and the Christian family build up the Church: for in the family the human person is not only brought into being and progressively introduced by means of education into the human community, but by means of the rebirth of baptism and education in the faith the child is also introduced into God's family, which is the Church."[1]

It is interesting to recall that the early Church began its life in meetings at Christian homes and gatherings of families. Th e coming together of different families began to make up the larger family of God, sharing all things in common.[2] Th e family of God's people who come together under the umbrella of the same Father are therefore, even in these days of severe individualism, only recognizable and fully identifiable in the unity of all her individual family units.

Now these individual family units are not perfect units. The United States Bishops' Conference had reflected and offered succinct words to describe the nature of the Christian family. "A family is holy not because it is perfect, but because God's grace is at work in it, helping it to set out anew everyday on the way of love."[3]

No family better illustrates the last point better than the holy family of Jesus, Mary and Joseph. From issues about the paternity of Jesus and the wonderful ways in which he was born which must have given rise to lots of challenges amongst Mary's contemporaries; to the early life of the new born babe with whom the holy family had to flee

---

[1] John Paul II, *Familiaris Consortio, On the role of the Christian Family in the modern world*, (1981), 15.

[2] See Acts of Apostles 4:32

[3] United State Conference of Catholic Bishops, *Follow the Way of* Love, Pastoral message of the U.S. Catholic Bishops to Families, 1994.

to Egypt; to the myriad of scenes, maybe a bit confusing for Mary and Joseph, that played out in the early life of this wonderful baby[4], the holy family witnesses to the possibility of holiness in spite of the several upheavals that could abound. The aforementioned challenges to the holy family highlight the several challenges that still beset human families of today.

Perhaps those challenges can be argued to be heightened in our contemporary days. With more fundamental challenges to the nature of the family, divisive thoughts on what makes up a family, the debate on the necessity of the family for the healthy wholeness of the society and other such challenges, there is no gainsaying that the value of the family is passing through a most heated kiln of trial.

Like many other moral dilemmas that we face, and as it is the case with several Christian practices which sometimes come under questioning and fire, the Church continues to echo the mind of Christ on the purpose of the creator and the essence of the family. This is one of those grey areas of human values for which the body of Christ has suffered several blows and criticisms. But I do not think a soft approach to the issue clears away all the difficulties. The truth remains that issues of family life, being the foundational issues from which others are spawned, would continue to generate much attention, deliberation and oftentimes disagreement. It is understandable.

When Jesus, for instance, taught such a knotty doctrine about divorce, it did not go down well with what we could refer to as "the expectation of his day." Teachings on the family in our contemporary day would therefore continue to have its own furore. But the body of Christ, the Church, must like a mother continue to give direction and moral leadership even as humanity advances daily towards a

---

[4]   For instance the experience of his parents looking for their lost child for the three days only to be asked the heart rending question "why were you looking for me?", See Luke 3:41-50.

deeper appreciation of the divine design, and towards a continual understanding of the mysteries of the human person.

In any case, the Scripture sets before us the example of the holy family as a model, for instance in the Lucan text.[5] The adversities, tensions, mis-comprehensions often touted as causes of marriage difficulties and eventual breakdowns have also been lived by this family. The difference is the charity with which the two initial members of the holy family, Joseph and Mary, lived out their vision of the family, yielding to each other in love. A return to school at the threshold of the holy family would therefore seem to be a good idea for all families.

---

[5]   *Ibid.*

26

Mary, Help of Christians

> We never give more honour to Jesus than when we honour his Mother, and we honour her simply and solely to honour him all the more perfectly. We go to her only as a way leading to the goal we seek - Jesus, her Son.
> -Saint Louis Marie de Montfort,
> True Devotion to the Blessed Virgin, #94.

You probably know the joke of the boy who asked God for a bicycle as a gift at Christmas. He was full of optimism as the birthday of Christ approached. He kept looking under the Christmas tree everyday till the 24th of December but none of the wrapped gifts resembled a bicycle. Immediately after the midnight Mass, he rushed home hoping his bicycle would have arrived at least now at the saviour's birth. There was nothing like a bicycle. He had a last hope it would arrive the next day, the Boxing Day, and so woke up early and was the first in the living room. Yet there was no sign of a bicycle.

In disappointment the little boy sobbed all the way back to his bedroom. He had just had his first communion that year and had been told of the efficacy of prayers to Jesus, but apparently Jesus was not interested in giving him a bicycle, he thought. As he walked disappointedly to the bedroom to mourn his discontent with Jesus, he passed by his grandmother's room typically adorned with all sorts of statues, prayer cards, rosaries and candles. The little boy took a glance at all these ornaments of prayers, hissed and was to pass on to his bedroom. But at some thoughts he stopped short, returned to grandma's room, grabbed a statue of Mary and ran to his bedroom. After hiding the statue safely under his bed, he looked up and with a tone of confidence said, "Jesus, give me a bicycle or you will not see your mother again!"

The reaction of the boy in his frustration is hilarious. But the foundational reason for such a reaction is not merely hilarious, it is didactic. It is a realization of the importance of Mary to Jesus and the connection of that importance to salvation history. The Scripture bears us witness about this connection. At a time when Jesus himself avowed that he was not quite ready to begin his ministry and miracles, it took the intercession of Mary to avert a situation of shame and embarrassment for the newly wedded couple in Cana, Galilee. Her intercession changed the course of things even as Jesus changed jars of water into wine.[1] With the intercession of "the blessed amongst women", Jesus gave the very first sign which marked the beginning of his ministry.

The mystery of Mary as a major link to the saviour could never be overemphasized. Hans Urs Von Balthasar and Joseph Cardinal Ratzinger have shown us the intricate bond that exists between the salvific mission of Christ and the choice of Mary as a conduit for the saviour.[2] Mary did not just accept to bear the Saviour with her fiat. Her

---

[1]   John 2:1-11

[2]   See Hans Urs Von Balthasar and Joseph Cardinal Ratzinger, *Mary, the*

acceptance of the motherhood role made her the rich soil into which the virile seed was planted, a soil which yielded grains in its hundreds. The nature of that good soil therefore cannot possibly be disconnected from the virility of the grain. The intercessory nature of Mary is a constant in the Christian conception of her maternal role. It is this same intercessory role that the Church, the body of Christ, lives out in her witness to the risen saviour. The Church is equally fruitful when "she becomes holy soil for the Word"[3], offering life to the world and thus engaging in an intercessory "Marian mystery". In making His choice of a mode to endow the world with the gift of the saviour, God chose Mary. And Christ, in perpetuating his ministry on earth amongst us, chose his Church as the instrument of salvation. The mystery of Mary as the source of grace and that of the Church as an instrument of salvation are therefore both united in the person of Christ in whom alone is our salvation.

The Christian who is serious about his faith would necessarily be serious about the mystery of Mary as the help of Christians. Through her, the sun of salvation has broken upon our darkness. From this simple Jewish peasant girl it has pleased God to be born and nurtured in the person of Jesus. If Mary could change the mind of Jesus toward helping the couple at Cana, it would be a smart thing to be close to this woman and seek her intercession. Somewhat, that little boy was right to assume that Jesus would go out of his way to please us for Mary's sake.

Church at the Source, (Rome: Libreria Editrice Vaticana, 1997), p. 14ff.

[3]   *Ibid.* p. 17.

27

$\mathcal{B}aptism$

You cannot have forgotten that all of us, when we were baptized into Christ Jesus, were baptized into his death. So by our baptism into his death we were buried with him, so that as Christ was raised from the dead by the Father's glorious power, we too should begin living a new life.

-Romans 6:3-4

Two good friends, a Catholic and a Baptist, were conversing about the correct way of administering baptism. "So one is not baptized if the water only reaches his knee?" asked the Catholic. "No way. He has to be entirely immersed in the water" replied the Baptist. And the Catholic, "But what if the water reaches as high as his eyes, would that be enough?" Getting a little bit irritated, the Baptist retorted, "No. He has to be completely immersed, nothing short of that." With a knowing nod, the Catholic consented and said, "Yes, I guess we agree on the essential point then." Bewildered, the Baptist asked, "You mean you now believe proper baptism is by complete immersion?" This time around it was the turn of the Catholic to say "No." And continued, "but it seems we both agree that the sufficient condition for baptism is for water to touch one's head!"

Arguments on what form of baptism is best may be important, more important however is the recognition of the new reality that comes into being whenever the sacrament is celebrated. The Church defines the nature of this new reality as a "configuration to Christ" since this sacrament "seals the Christian with the indelible spiritual mark (*character*) of his belonging to Christ."[1]

Hence by Baptism, we enter into the life of Christ who underwent the grave but only to resurrect and bring life to his loved ones. With the waters of baptism we become a new creature, washed clean by the blood of the lamb. We gain the new life in Christ of which Paul was very fond of writing.[2] This new life has a pattern of positive radicalism. The newly baptized is assumed to leave behind an ignorant manner of living[3], to a life informed by values.[4] Such a change in a pattern of living for a baptized has even been described in more radical terms by St. Caesarius of Arles. He says "before baptism we were all shrines of the devil: baptized we have become temples of Christ."[5]

That indeed seems a bit stringent to the ears particularly if we reflect and remember, as someone argued, that all were created by God and for God and not for the devil. But the point of St. Caesarius is well made. It is an emphasis on the novelty to which the baptized is now called, a call into light from darkness.[6] A call into an inner life of the Spirit leading to informed actions as against a life lived solely in the flesh and with a presumption that man is the exclusive custodian of

---

1   *Catechism of the Catholic Church*, 1272.
2   See 2 Corinthians 5:17-19
3   Colossians 3:9
4   1 Corinthians 6:19-20, Romans 12:1
5   St. Caesarius of Arles, Sermon 229 I-3 in, the Second Reading, Divine Office, Feast of the Dedication of the Lateran Basilica, (November 9).
6   1 Peter 2:9

his own life, makes his own choices and lives by his own rule. No, the baptized no longer lives a life according to the prism of his own vision but as enlightened by the Spirit of Christ.[7]

If by this important sacrament which the Church calls "the gateway to life in the Spirit and the door which gives access to other sacraments"[8] we enter into the life of Christ, it is obvious that there must be concomitant obligations. The Christian born into new life by the cleansing waters of baptism has enormous obligations as much as he has a new status of rights and grace. It is only in the evidence of practical witnessing that the baptized lends credence to the new life he has received. That new life is gradually learnt and entered into, with a gradual growth into maturity in Christ.

To be baptized, from the Greek word *baptizo*, which means "immerse" or "be plunged into" is therefore to become fully immersed in the life of Christ, old things are passed away and a new life is there to see. It is to begin life anew with a novel reference-point located in Christ. If today there are stigmas in the life of the Church, it is because there are discrepancies between the actions of the baptized and the life of Christ. It is for that reason that Mahatma Gandhi is said to have told the great Stanley Jones, a Christian missionary to India, that he liked Christ but not Christians because "Christians are so unlike your Christ."[9]

Our baptism is a call to the same life Christ lived and to an upholding of the same values he taught. If we are to be exemplary as baptized Christians then we shall have to imbibe those same values.

---

[7] Romans 8:1-13

[8] *Op. Cit.*, 1213.

[9] See James Edward Stroud, *The Knights Templar and the Protestant Reformation, The Case for a Modern-Day Monk*, (Maitland: Xulon Press, 2011), p. 162.

$\mathcal{R}$evisiting that early love

Love is always patient and kind; ... It is always ready to make
allowances, to trust, to hope and to endure whatever comes.
-1 Corinthians 13: 4-7

Henry Ford, the great American automobile entrepreneur was once
asked to share the secret behind his successful marriage. His reply was
simple, "It is the same secret behind my success in the car business. I
stick to one model."

The stability landscape of marriages in contemporary time is
obviously not looking good. And the more years pass by, the higher
the statistics of broken marriages and separated spouses. Sad as this
development is, the problem is not quite amenable to an easy solution
or to a simple apportioning of blame to this or that party. In our
society which is different from the past societies in ways more than
one, values which encourage divorce continue to be reinforced. Hence
it is sometimes not even the desire of a good number of couples to go

separate ways, they simply find themselves in the whirlpool of societal value-upheavals.

Be that as it may however, the uncompromising stance of Christ on the issue of divorce remains the ultimate ideal for the Christian.[1] It is the same ideal which the Church of God has always promoted and defended. And even though the Church of God recognizes the pain that could sometimes arise in the union of man and woman, yet she is not oblivious to the agony of divorce which "introduces disorder into the family and into the society. This disorder brings grave harm to the deserted spouse, to children traumatized by the separation of their parents and often torn between them, and because of its contagious effect which makes it truly a plague on society."[2]

Hence, while recognizing situations in which a spouse is unjustly abandoned in spite of numerous efforts to prevent same[3], the Church argues for the need to actively promote the preservation of the matrimonial bond.

A journey of a thousand miles, as the saying goes, starts with a step forward. In trying to combat the downward spiral of the success rate of marriages, it is necessary to identify the root causes of divorces in our contemporary society and reflect on ways in which such causes can be either uprooted or, in the worst scenario, mitigated so that they have less potent effects on the entire edifice of marriage. Of the many possible causes, we shall focus on just one in this reflection. It is a focus on the failure to "yield to each other" in a relationship, especially such a relationship as important as a marriage.

Points of views are always means of self-expression, yes. But they are not necessarily means of sustaining a relationship. Since these two who have been made one by virtue of marriage now live a common life in a union of love, there is the necessity of being able to yield to each

---

[1] Matthew 5:31-32; 19:3-9; Mark 10:9; Luke 16:18
[2] *Catechism of the Catholic Church*, 2385.
[3] *Ibid.*, 2386.

other when points of view do differ. And invariably, points of view do differ a lot. When Paul, giving a general exhortation to the Philippians, commended them to "be of the same mind"[4], he was not expecting some magic to happen and make different people conform to each other in such a way that their personal views and points of view concur always. That would not even be beneficial to relationships as experience teaches us that diversity of views enriches our lives than a monotony of unexamined thoughts.

Thus it would seem the ability of the couples who began their married life some thirty years ago to recognize their differences, and their readiness to defer to each other when such differences manifest, is a key instrument which has helped in stabilizing their unions. Contemporary marriages tend to suffer cracks and break-ups when such a readiness to "yield" to each other is lacking.

In our present efficient and rights-conscious social milieu, the virtue of patience which is one of the fruits of the Holy Spirit has to be further sought and extolled. That fruit commends us to a life of thoughtfulness and tolerance. The King James Version of the scriptural verse from which the Church compiled the list of the fruits of the Holy Spirit actually referred to patience as "long-suffering".[5] A mutual yielding to each other's perspectives, a "long-suffering" with each other, is an essential element which was characteristic of marriages of years past but is under fire in contemporary marriages. It is an element that has to be revisited.

It is true that feminism has done a lot of good, making significant changes to male-chauvinism in our world. But we would be making the same mistake if the evil or bad-practice of male-chauvinism swings the pendulum to become female-chauvinism. Both do not have a legitimate nor moral stance in Christian life.

---

[4]   Philippians 2:2
[5]   See Galatians 5:22-23, King James Version.

While there are many other developments that we could identify as causes for marriage break-ups, the inability of contemporary couples to yield to each other in patience would seem primal. Thoughtfulness for and tolerance of the other are virtues to be revisited if the spate of divorce is to be abated. After all, the "two" who became "one" were not initially one. The sacramental oneness which is achieved in a day could only possibly be learnt and lived out in time. Patience and yielding to each other in love is the ultimate word to stability in marriage.

29

Epiphany of the Lord

We saw his star as it rose and we have come to do him homage

-Matthew 2:2

The word epiphany is from the Greek *"epiphaneia"*, manifestation, itself from *epiphainein* "to show". The essential focus of epiphany of the Lord is his manifestation to all peoples. At Christmas we celebrate the birth of Jesus, rejoicing that he who has come that we may have life and have it to the full is born for us.[1] The dawn of salvation breaks upon us in the birth of the saviour. But the epiphany has a focus different from the celebration of Christmas. The epiphany celebrates the coming of the light of the entire world, the coming of He who is to be made known to all nations. His reign extends from one end of the earth to the other, a reign which will have no end.[2]

---

[1] John 10:10
[2] Isaiah 9:7

The manifestation of Jesus to the world was understandably very interesting. Right from this manifestation, the stage was already well-set to make us understand that this child was born for all. Even though the Jews waited expectantly for the Messiah, it was more of an expectation of a warring King who would, and understandably so, "deliver them from their enemies." Thus being born in some hut amidst animals was the last scene they expected. But much less expected was the welcome team for this long-awaited Messiah. First, he was welcomed and adored by the simplest of all hearts, the shepherds.[3] Shepherds would typically not be amongst people expected to welcome the saviour since they were ordinarily considered unclean and needed to undergo special purification to enable then partake in temple worship. Yet it was to them that the angels revealed the good news of the new born child.

And then Jesus was visited by three wise men from the orient. These magi, who searched the heavens for signs and read the stars for information did not only come from the east (an illustration of how far off they were from Bethlehem, the birth place of Jesus), but were essentially a representation of the gentile world. In the visitation of the new born by these two groups of people, the evangelists presented to us some novelty about the expected Messiah: he is born for all, to be manifested to all, and to save all. As St. Paul succinctly puts it, in Jesus the old barrier which used to separate peoples in disparate groups has been broken down and humanity has been united in his person.[4]

This awesome development of the manifestation of Jesus to all and his unification of all peoples by his coming has tremendous implications for us as Christians. The light of his manifestation shines upon our darkness and enlightens our vision to see in clearer dimensions the plans of God who calls the whole of humanity into a brotherhood and sisterhood. The Kingship of Jesus is a sovereignty which extends to all races, languages, and peoples; it

---

[3]   Luke 2:1-19

[4]   Ephesians 2:14

is a reign which unifies all divisions and separations. By logical conclusion, it is a reign which calls us too to a unified vision of the people of God. Nobody is meant to be considered as excluded from the flock of God, for he works as He wills and chooses as it pleases him. This knowledge needs to inform our relationship with people. Naturally we have our preferences in life. Much as that is true, those preferences do not have to reflect a scorn for others not so preferred. One of the simple messages of the epiphany is that we are saved by grace and called to life by He who mercifully reached out to us while we were far.

The manifestation of Christ to all also commends us to a greater adhesion to his person; it calls us to a dependence on the insightful illumination that comes from this "light of all nations". In going about our choices in life, several decisions could be quite difficult. There are lots of times when all seem dark and dreary. Particularly at those times when we are faced by life-size options, and are confused about what path to tread. At such times we need to remember the amazing gift we have in Jesus, the daystar which enlightens all hearts. He has been manifested to all not only for us to see his glory but by the light of that glory, to be constantly illumined and guided along the trajectory of wisdom.

30

$\mathcal{P}$entecost

Come Holy Spirit fill the hearts of your faithful, and
enkindle in them the power of your love.
Send forth your Spirit and they shall be created, and you
will renew the face of the earth

There is a beautiful observation made by St. John Chrysostom about the beginnings of Christianity. In his homilies on the first letter to the Corinthians he wrote "See how the folly of God is wiser than men, and his weakness stronger. How is it stronger? In that it [the gospel] overran the whole world and gripped all men, and although countless people were trying to obliterate the name of the Crucified, the contrary happened. It flowered and grew larger, but they perished and withered, and the living who were fighting against him who had died did not prevail....What tax gatherers and fishermen had strength to achieve by the grace of God, that neither kings nor orators nor philosophers, not, in a word, the whole world searching in all directions, could even imagine....Here were men who failed to stand up to the Jews when Christ was alive. Yet when he died and was buried they arrayed themselves against the whole world."[1]

The principal agent responsible for this unbelievable difference in the actions of the apostles immediately after the death of Christ on the one hand, and after his resurrection on the other, is the Holy Spirit. The scriptures recall that just after the death of Christ, "...the doors were closed in the room where the disciples were, for fear of the Jews."[2] The natural fear which cripples the mind of the human person from reaching out and achieving some good was at work in the apostles. Indeed, the words of the Scriptures, "I shall strike the shepherd and the sheep of the flock will be scattered"[3] were already fulfilled.

The eleven (with the unfortunate omission of Judas Iscariot who had gone "...to his proper place"[4]) must have reasoned amongst themselves about the absurdity of trying to continue the mission of Jesus who apparently had failed them. The Messiah was dead, that is an irony the apostles could never have understood even if they tried. Usually the Messiah saves, he does not die. And even while the risen saviour conversed with them on the way to Emmaus, the reality of what had transpired in the last few days so numbed their minds to believe any further good could be done about the mission of Jesus.

It took the coming of the Holy Spirit, sent by the Father in fulfilment of the promise of Jesus, to warm up their numb minds and "remind them of all that he had taught them." The Pentecost cleared the fear and cowardice of the apostles in the face of the threat of the elders of the time who had connived to put their master to death. With the

---

[1]   See John Chrysostom, Homilies on the first letter of the Corinthians, in *The Office of Readings*, Feast of St. Bartholomew, Apostle, (August 24).
[2]   John 20:19
[3]   Matthew 26:31
[4]   Acts of Apostles 1:25

coming of the Holy Spirit at Pentecost, the otherwise cold and fearful apostles spoke "...as the Spirit gave them power to express themselves."[5]

The scene and reality of the Pentecost would ever be relevant for the Christian of today and tomorrow even as it was for the apostles. Even though the good news directs us in the way of truth and the way that leads to life, the ideals of the faith could sometimes be so overwhelming as to make even the most fervent of hearts cold. The moral currents of our society could bear such a strong tide as to sweep us away when difficult situations emerge. Our own personal struggles could also be so compelling that sometimes we could erroneously be tempted to consider an abandonment of the "Way, the Truth and Life" as an easier option. In such circumstances, nothing short of the power that comes from on high could keep the Christian going.

The snag sometimes on our way in the full embrace of the Holy Spirit is a preconception of where He is taking us or what He is able to do. Both preconceptions are useless as they are limiting. For one, the Spirit of truth always takes us to great places, much more than we can imagine just as was the case with the apostles. A day after the death of Christ, nobody could have convinced them that the Word would be preached in all languages and understood by all heart that listened. And on the other count, the Holy Spirit is the third person of the Trinity and thus omnipotent. Nothing is too powerful for Him to accomplish. That was the assurance that the Angel Gabriel gave to Mary at the incipience of our salvation history, "for nothing is impossible to God.[6] That remains the assurance that keeps the believer going.

---

5   Acts of Apostles 2:4
6   Luke 1:37

31

Good Works

If one of the brothers or one of the sisters is in need of clothes and has not enough food to live on, and one of you says to them 'I wish you well; keep yourself warm and eat plenty', without giving them these bare necessities of life, then what good is that? In that same way faith, if good deeds do not go with it, is quite dead.

-James 2:14-17

Children have a real simplistic but beautiful view of life. This simplicity permeates how they perceive others and how they relate to others generally. A teacher of a Sunday school liturgy for children discovered this simplicity in a shocking manner while teaching a class about the last four things. "If I sold my house and my car, had a big garage sale and gave all my money to the church, would that get me into Heaven?" he asked the children. "NO!" the children all answered. "If I cleaned the church every day, mowed the yard, and kept everything neat and tidy, would that get me into Heaven?" Again, the answer was, "NO!" "Well, then, if I was kind to animals and gave candy to all the children and loved my wife, would that get me into Heaven?" the teacher asked them again. Again, they all answered, "NO!" "Well," the teacher continued, "then how can I get into Heaven?" A six-year-old boy shouted out, "you gotta be dead!" The poor teacher was trying to teach a lesson on the necessity of faith and good works.

St. James had written beautifully on the lesson which the teacher was trying to pass on to the children. "Faith, if good deeds do not go with it, is quite dead", taught James.[1] There are several laws and precepts that guide human and Christian conduct. Fidelity to the faith requires that these laws are obeyed and the precepts kept. Our road to heaven is a gradual march of daily steps. But much as keeping of laws and precepts are important, they would be null and void if what Jesus referred to as "the weightier matters of the law" were neglected.[2] Good works which manifest themselves in justice, mercy and love are the hallmarks of a true respect for the commandments of God and needed actions to march a desire for heaven.

Jesus always pointed out the importance of esoteric (internal) practice of religion as against an exoteric (external) "display" of religious acts. Whereas an esoterically religious person internalizes the dictates of religion and turns them into guiding principles for a life well lived, the exoteric believer merely practices religion as an observance of rituals and external code of behaviour. Jesus never spared calling any of such external show of religion by its name: a hypocrisy which does not take anybody anywhere.[3] Real faith is only exemplified by good works; there can be no true faith without accompanying good deeds. It is a Christian teaching which St. Paul had expressed in an as-a-matter-of-fact and curt language in his ode to love. It is in good deeds, which are invariably the product of love, that testimony is rendered to true faith and an aspiration for heaven is adequately pursued.

---

[1]   James 2:17
[2]   Matthew 23:23
[3]   See Matthew 23

The consequence is that there are several religious/spiritual practices that we may embark on in life but they cannot take the place of the simple request of Christ, "In truth I tell you, in so far as you did this to one of the least of these brothers of mine, you did it to me."[4] It is for the same reason that the Church does not teach the spiritual works of mercy while neglecting the corporal works of mercy. Both go hand-in-hand, complementing each other in a manner of necessity rather than in exclusivity. In his insightful book on works of mercy, Mark Shea succinctly presents to us why it is that spiritual works of mercy would be found wanton if not complemented by the corporal works of mercy; and why it is that corporal works of mercy could turn out to be mere heroism that lacks the necessary underlying divine dimension if the spiritual works of mercy are left out of consideration. Both must be active in a Christian's life if we are to "incarnate our faith in works of love for God and neighbour".[5]

The exigency of uniting faith with good works is not only apparent to us from the admonition of Christ "It is not anyone who says to me, 'Lord, Lord', who will enter the kingdom of heaven, but the person who does the will of my Father in heaven."[6] It is also discernible from reason. If I preached the gospel the whole day and got back home only to nag at all persons and possibly all things around me, it is evident that there is a lot of disconnect. Or if I gave out large sum of money in charity but would not spare a miserable guy who made a mistake and craves my indulgence for a pardon, a gaping hole is visible in my overall spirituality. Our path to heaven shall be built not only by our important "Hail Marys", but also by our good works through which our salt would not lose its taste but spice the world.

---

[4]   Matthew 25:40
[5]   Mark Shea, *The Work of Mercy: Being the Hands and Heart of Christ*, (Cincinnati: Servant Books, 2011), p. 9.
[6]   Matthew 17:21

Does God Exist?

The fool has said in his heart, 'there is no God.' (Psalm 14:1)

The most important considerations within the Christian faith do not appear to stand on the sturdiest of foundations. The question of the existence of God, which is the most meaningful question an atheist would pose when issues of religion arise, seems to be a formidable question for us Christians. It is a question which has spanned thousands of years and has been reformulated in different ways. Several great Christian minds have debated this phenomenon and confronted its difficulty. Amongst them great minds like Thomas Aquinas, Augustine and Bonaventure have offered explanations and proofs of the existence of God. But even the best of the arguments of these fine minds have their limitations. Crucial amongst such limitations is the poser raised by atheists on the sub-question on the existence of evil. Augustine (and later Aquinas) would reply to such an objection and say the question of evil does not negate the existence of God because evil is a "nothing", a privation or an absence of what should be there, and so it is not something created by God but an absence of a good. The counter from unbelievers and, more so, by believers who have suffered great evil like the loss of an entire family would be "even if it is a privation and a 'nothing', why would such a very good and powerful and all-knowing God omit such a good?" It is obvious that attempting the proofs of the existence of God merely on physical, human terms would always suffer some rational deadlock.

Thus, setting out to prove the existence of God in its entirety remains a tall dream for the human mind. The fact remains that the question of the existence of God is not squarely a question in the "proof domain", nor is it a phenomenon subject to scientific discovery. After all is said and done, in spite of the many proofs that attempt to explain the mystery, the existence of God remains an article of faith and a mystery per excellence.

But be that as it may, Christians are encouraged to always have answers ready "for people who ask you the reason for the hope that you have"[1] The arguments for the existence of God from the beauty of design, or from the necessity of a great mind/being who must have created are awesome. But, as we have seen, they are limited. The best arguments would however seem to come from the testimonies of individual lives. They come from individual chronicles of the movement of this great being in our personal lives and in great ways that are short of explanation.

The fact that one cannot give an unquestionable physical argument for the existence of God is not enough evidence that He does not exist. Negating the existence of God because of the impossibility of flawlessly proving same is nothing short of falling into the very error of which atheists accuse believers. One could even say it would be unscientific to write-off belief in this great being that we refer to as God just because of our impossibility to give a flawless argument for his existence, whereas there are several realities indicating to us such an existence.

---

[1]   1 Peter 3:15

The story about a simple inference made by a Christian whose faith was being assailed by an atheist-barber is instructive here. The Christian had gone to a barbershop to have his hair cut and his beard trimmed. As the barber began to work, they began to have a good conversation. They talked about so many things and various subjects. When they eventually touched on the subject of God, the barber said: "I don't believe that God exists." "Why do you say that?" asked the customer. "Well, you just have to go out in the street to realize that God doesn't exist. Tell me, if God exists, would there be so many sick people? Would there be abandoned children? If God existed, there would be neither suffering nor pain. I can't imagine a loving God who would allow all of these things."

The customer thought for a moment, but didn't respond because, for one he didn't want to start an argument, and secondly his faith actually received a salvo of uncertainty from the barber's assertions. The barber finished his job and the customer left the shop. Just after he left the barbershop, he saw a man in the street with long, stringy, dirty hair and an untrimmed beard. He looked dirty and unkempt. The customer turned back, entered the barbershop again and said to the barber: "You know what? Barbers do not exist." "How can you say that?" asked the surprised barber. "I am here, and I am a barber. And I just worked on you!" "No!", the customer exclaimed. "Barbers don't exist because if they did, there would be no people with dirty long hair and untrimmed beards, like that man outside." "Ah, but barbers DO exist! That's what happens when people do not come to me." "Exactly!", affirmed the customer. "That's the point! God, too, DOES exist! That's what happens when people do not go to Him and don't look to Him for full understanding of the realities of life." And those realities are often too complicated for our mind which perceive in simplistic, materialistic manner.

On the final analysis, the issue of the existence of God is not a proof issue. It is an issue of faith in He in whom "we live, and move, and exist."[2]

---

[2]   Acts of Apostles 17:28.

33

When is the End of Time?

As believers, we are already with the Lord in our lifetime;
our future, eternal life, has already begun.

-Benedict XVI,
General Audience 12 November, 2008.

Even as I write the media is still awash with the news of the Nov 8, 2013 devastation in the Philippines, the so-called super typhoon Haiyan. The disastrous storm-surge has already claimed over 3,000 lives, and still counting. May their souls rest in peace, and may the Lord grant consolation to the bereaved, solace to the afflicted.

President Barrack Obama, in his initial message of condolence and solidarity on the incident, remarked that the disaster is "a heartbreaking reminder of how fragile life is." That remark goes straight into the heart of the Christian faith, even if the President had made it in a social-cultural context. It underscores the fragility of human existence, the little difference between prosperity and paucity, the short difference between life and death.

The question about when the end of time shall come is equally connected to recognition of this fragility of human existence. At a time when people watched the heavily decorated temple of Jerusalem with mouth-gaping astonishment, Jesus called attention to the temporariness of all those decorations, indeed to the temporariness of the entire temple itself.[1] His prophecy came to pass: the temple of Jerusalem was destroyed in the year 70AD.

The evangelist Luke who gave us this account had a greater lesson to unveil to his readers about the intention of Jesus. A very important key to reading that section of the gospel is "Your perseverance will win you your lives."[2] Thus, even though Jesus, as presented by Luke, had spoken about the end of time in very fearful and apocalyptic language as reflective of the mode of understanding of the time, he continually warned of the need not to be deceived by signs,[3] "for this is something that must happen first, but the end will not come at once."[4]

Therefore rather than a push along the lines of anxiety and fear as suggested by the cosmic language in use here, Jesus on the final analysis prompted his listeners to having a discerning attitude, and to standing their ground in spite of the apparent chaos and cosmic disorder.

One basic way to having such a discerning attitude is the ability to realize that getting prepared for the end of time is not achieved by anxieties or unnecessary worries. Thoughts about the end of time naturally bring anxieties and worries. Taking into consideration that "the span of our life is seventy years, eighty for those who are strong"[5] makes us think deeply of the place where we shall spend eternity. It

---

[1]   Luke 21:5-19
[2]   Luke 21:19
[3]   Luke 21:7-8
[4]   Luke 21:9
[5]   Psalm 90:10

equally makes us wonder when it is that Christ would come again as taught by the scriptures.

The exhortation of Jesus to us about the end of time is for us to be perseverant in hope and live our actual life presently well. On the final analysis, a Christian life is not lived merely in expectation of the end. If that were the sole reason for living, the Christian could not possibly be the salt of this earth and light of this world. The Christian's life is fruitful and meaningful when such a life touches on the lives of others and fructifies the seeds of aspiration and needs of many in whose proximity it finds itself. That is why the Baltimore Catechism would not define the reason why God created us as merely "being with Him in Heaven" alone. It rather says God created us "to know Him, to love Him, and to serve Him in this world" and only after that "to be happy with Him forever in heaven."[6] This is in sync with Jesus' appeal not to be overtaken by the anxieties of the end time or about when the Son of man shall come the second time.

It is no wonder then that when St. Francis of Assisi was asked what he would do if he were to learn the world would end this very evening he replied, "I would try and finish what I am doing right now." At that point in time Francis was actually hoeing his garden.

We are called to a patient dedication to the care of the life which God has blessed us with here on earth, even as we look forward to the arrival of his reign someday known to him alone. The best preparation for the end of time is a peaceful living-out of today, and tomorrow and the next.

---

[6] See Baltimore Catechism, First Lesson, Question 6.

34

~~Truth in Charity~~

We must correct out of love, not out of a desire to hurt, but
with the loving intention of helping the person's amendment.
If we act like that, we will be fulfilling the commandment
very well – "if your brother sins against you, go and tell him
his fault, between you and him alone." Why do you correct
him? Because you are upset that he has offended you? God
forbid. If you do it out of self-love, your action is worthless. If
it is love that moves you, you are acting excellently.

-St. Augustine, Sermon 82,4.

Consider these two scenarios. First: a lady is known for her wayward
attitude. She has a Christian neighbour next to her apartment who is so
appalled by her ways that she (the neighbour) would pass by this other
lady of easy virtues every morning without a greeting, give a bad look,
mutter out the words "you better repent" and hiss on her way out, to
complete her demonstration of utter disgust.

Second: a lady is known for her wayward attitude. She has a Christian neighbour next to her apartment who is shocked at her behaviours. But every morning while passing by the lady of easy virtues, the Christian neighbour would give a little smile, and occasionally stop to say a short hello.

Now supposing there arose the need to propose the good news of the gospel to this wayward lady to which of the neighbours would she be most willing to listen? You are right in mentioning the courteous, smiling neighbour. The fact is that sentiments of care and love are attractive; whereas an attitude of harsh condemnation and discourteous piety are always repulsive.

It is this same sentiment that we witness in the attitude of Jesus to his contemporaries. In his mission to the world, Jesus did not mince words in saying he had come to save sinners. Just like the doctor was not needed by a healthy person but by the sick, Jesus knew it was the sinner that needed him more than the righteous.[1] But how would the saviour have been effective in bringing the message of repentance and hope to such sinners (the greatest of which St. Paul claims to be)[2] if he had not broken through the thick wall of segregation and disregard which kept the sinners at bay from the righteous?

That wall of segregation and disregard would always be a stumbling block to the work of evangelization. The only hammer which can dislodge it is the hammer of truth prudently, albeit eloquently, spoken in charity. Charity is the first law and the most important law. All other precepts revolve round it and pass through it. Lost as a value, all other precepts lose their value.

A lot of people were taking aback when Benedict XVI unveiled the title of his first encyclical as a Pope. An ingenious mind of incalculable value to the theoretical formulation of laws, decrees and doctrines of the Church, many had expected an encyclical of a highly theological

---

[1]   Matthew 9:11-13
[2]   1 Timothy 1:15

and speculative nature from the erstwhile Joseph Ratzinger. This was not the case as the Pope wrote an encyclical titled "God is love." His second encyclical was on hope, and the third encyclical makes a return to the theme of love and fraternal correction and is titled "Charity in truth." This sequence of writings which revolved around love was not arbitrary or by accident. It was a conscious choice of the Pope at the time to dwell on the most important Christian value in our world "where the name of God is sometimes associated with vengeance or even a duty of hatred and violence."[3] For it is only a heart which is shown much love that has the possibility of hearing the call of love.

There is no gainsaying that a lot of values need fixing in our world. But that fixing would only be accepted, respected and effected within the ambience of charity, a charity which eventually lightens up the alley of life and makes it gleam with adornments of truth. The fundamental dilemma for the Christian in giving good examples or in being the salt of the earth and light of the world is how to balance the chasm between truth and charity. That chasm is not necessary – and that is an understatement – the chasm in fact undermines the possibility of repentance of many who have strayed but need more than a harsh reprimand in order to find their way back to the fold.

In conclusion it is important to remember the very source of all good and the one who is calling to conversion. It is God himself whose definition is essentially love. Thus any correction offered to an erring individual can only be valid if done with that definition in perspective. For at one time or the other "we too were ignorant",[4] living some sort of life not perfectly compatible with the gospel, occasions we generally refer to as sins. The love shown to us by God on those occasions therefore necessitates our reaching out to others with no less charity and understanding.

3   Benedict XVI, Encyclical Letter *Deus Caritas Est, On Christian Love*, December 25, 2005.

4   Titus 3:3

35

Courage!

All great masters are chiefly distinguished by the power of adding a second, a third, and perhaps a fourth step in a continuous line. Many a man had taken the first step. With every additional step you enhance immensely the value of your first.

-Ralph Waldo Emerson

Have you ever felt so afraid that you sometimes dread making more efforts to go on? Are there times when your courage is at its lowest ebb and you feel like the entire world is falling on you? Do you sometimes wish you reach out for your dream and do the needful but the strength to do this fails you? Well then you are not alone! Yourself, myself, several million others and Jesus himself have been in the same situation. Yeah, you read right, even Jesus himself.

The episode which recounts the experience of Jesus in the garden of Gethsemane is not the brightest of all episodes, as far as the humanity of Jesus was concerned, even if for us it marked one of the most important moments of the story of salvation.[1] For through his agony and suffering we have been saved. As we do say during the *Via Crucis* (Way of the Cross), "we adore you o Lord and we praise you, for by your holy Cross you have redeemed the world."

But it is easier to laud the name of the Lord than to recount what he had to go through at that crucial time. The truth remains that it was a most difficult time even for Jesus who "offered up prayers and entreaty, with loud cries and with tears, to the one who had the power to save him from death."[2] His courage initially failed him and he wished "that the cup pass me by."[3]

This is equally our own experience at different times and in different contexts of life. Reflecting on the importance of courage, C.S. Lewis had written that "Courage is not simply one of the virtues but the form of every virtue at the testing point."[4] The best of things do not come naturally as one might expect them. They require some measure of consistent sacrifice, strength of purpose and courage. One simple way to point out the fact that good things in life require courage is the level of commitment and the sense of dedication that is found in any sector of life where successful individuals are found. Be they teachers, factory workers, doctors, office secretaries and even students, there is always a corresponding correlation between a sense of courage and excellence. The options in life that do not come with some levels of challenges are often not our best deal. Thus, the call to a courageous 'stand-up' in life is a call to excellence; it is a call to draw ourselves into full length in affronting challenges which, in the thinking of the great scientist Albert Einstein, are nothing but opportunities.

---

1   See Matthew 26:36-46; Luke 22:39-46; Mark 14:32-42

2   Hebrews 5:7

3   Matthew 26:39

4   Clive Staples Lewis, *The Screwtape Letters*, (New York: HarperCollins Publishers, 2000 ed.) p. 161.

It is an irony that it is at the very times when we face difficulties and our courage is put to the test that we experience great levels of growth in our lives. At this point, the difference is made between an achiever and a passive receiver. Take for instance the example of Ludwig Beethoven. History has it that the very best of his compositions were made at a time when he was practically struggling with deafness. A passive receiver would simply have given up in the face of such a challenge, but not Beethoven, an achiever. He is now remembered in history as one of the greatest composers of all time. The same can be said of the almost legendary Rosa Parks who, at a time that the United States and indeed the entire world was sprawled in the mud of racial discrimination, stood her grounds with courage by refusing to give up her seat in the bus in accordance with the law in force in Montgomery, Alabama. Though the scourge of racism is still very much with us, Parks' courageous action has already made tremendous impact in the society. Her singular courage marked the end of segregation along racial lines in the usage of public transport. We can remember many more inspiring persons who have taught us the same lesson that the path to excellence is the path of courage and diligence.

In essence therefore, the times of difficulties are not necessarily the worst of times for us. They have their silver linings and offer us opportunities to face the world with a more determined mindset. Indeed, the difficult takes a little while, the impossible a little longer.

36

Immanuel: God with Us

Look! The virgin is with child and will give birth to a son whom they will call Immanuel, a name which means 'God-is-with-us.' -Matthew 1:23

With the fall came a loss, a colossal one at that! Humanity, in Adam preferred a fruit to the entire garden.[1] That preference came with its consequences. Humanity lost accord with God, and the garden, the symbol of human-divine harmony was shut with angels stationed on its boundaries to prevent man any further interaction with the "bare divine". The book of Genesis paints a picture of a lost friendship, love went awry! God seems to be distanced from man in consequence of sin and the "*Deus absconditus*"[2] theorists seem to be justified. Yet, God

---

[1]   See Genesis 3

[2]   *Deus absconditus* (an absconded God) in its extreme understanding, is a theory which suggests that God created the universe and then abandoned it. Those who suggest such a theory point to the evil in the world. However the

whose name is love and ever present never abandoned man; even the fall will not alter his nature. As St. Paul puts it, "If we are faithless, he is faithful still, for he cannot disown his own self."[3] So much so that as he doled out the punishment to humanity in the loins of Adam and Eve, He also gave a promise of redemption through the "offspring" of the woman, in what biblical scholars call the *proto-evangelium* (the first gospel).[4] Friendship was lost but friendship was promised!

Mary, the new Eve, mother of the living, bore Jesus Christ, the God-made-man as the direct fulfillment of that prophecy. Paul the Apostle helps us to understand this mystery, when he says in Galatians 4:4-5, "... but when the appointed time had come, God sent his Son born of a woman, born a subject of the law, so that we could receive adoption as sons (and daughters)." Such is the mystery of Christmas when, true to his promise, the virgin conceived and bore a son and gave him the name Immanuel. The eternal Word of God became flesh and lived among us.[5] By taking flesh he exalts humanity which was grounded by sin; human flesh the instrument of the fall, became renewed and imbued with a promise of glorification.

At Christmas, the God who made the universe and holds it in existence freely chose to step into our history in a most unprecedented and mysterious fashion. For love of us his creatures, he chose to become one us so as to lift us up from our dunghill of sin; he was born an infant at Bethlehem in a manger among smelly sheep. St. Augustine puts it well when he says "the son of God became the son of man that the sons of men might become the son of God". Jesus was born to save his people, born to restore the lost friendship. His birth which we

---

expression has a slight and more constructive variant in the thoughts of some theologians like Martin Luther and Karl Barth who used it to indicate the "hiddeness of God" or the fact that God is beyond human comprehension but reveals himself by himself and as he decides.

3   2 Timothy 2:13
4   See Genesis 3:15
5   See John 1:14

commemorate at Christmas is therefore a new dawn for humanity. It is God's love song to humanity with outstretched hands. It is a joyful message that He's not done with us yet, He is ever at work in us.

With the birth of Christ, God spoke to us in the best language possible. St. John of the Cross says "in giving us his Son, ... (God) spoke everything to us at once in this sole word – and he has no more to say....because what he spoke before to the prophets in parts he has now spoken all at once by giving us the ALL who is his son."[6] No wonder human history takes its dating from his birth and is re-oriented by it. Now God's dwelling is among men, we are no longer alone. God in Christ is with us to face life's challenges and to journey with us. There is no need to live in fear for God is Immanuel!

In Christ we are put in direct touch with our God. The story of Christmas was at last understood by that woman who was seated by a fireplace, wondering why God ever decided to come in the flesh. The whole thing seemed so absurd. Why would God take flesh and live among us? Then she heard a noise outdoors. She saw a dozen geese groping about in the snow, cold and confused. She went outside and tried to herd them into her warm garage. But the more she tried to help them, the more they scattered across the lawn. Finally she gave up. Then an odd thought came to her: *if just for a minute I could become a goose and talk to them in their language, I could explain that what I was trying to do was for their happiness.* Then it struck her. *That's what Christmas is all about! It's about God becoming a human to teach us what is necessary for our happiness and to lead the way!*

---

[6] St. John of the Cross, *The Ascent of Mount Carmel* 2,22,3-5 in *The Collected Works of St. John of the Cross*, tr. K. Kavanaugh, OCD, and O. Rodriguez, OCD (Washington DC: Institute of Carmelite Studies, 1979).

37

He is Risen!

Alleluia! He is alive never more to die.

This conversation once ensued between a Christian and his Muslim neighbor. The Muslim said to the Christian, "We Muslims have one thing you Christians do not have. When we go to Medina, we find a coffin and know that Muhammad lived because his body is in it. But when you Christians go to Jerusalem, you find nothing but an empty tomb." "Thank you," replied the Christian. "What you say is absolutely true, and that makes the eternal difference. The reason we find an empty tomb is because we serve a risen Christ!"[1]

The resurrection of Christ which Easter celebrates remains a most central article of the Christian faith. No shade of Christianity would be worthy of the tag "Christian," without first professing that Jesus the Christ truly suffered, died, was buried and rose triumphant on

---

[1]   Roy Zuck, ed., The Speaker's Quote Book, (Grand Rapids: Kregel Publications, 1997), p. 436.

the third day; and never more to die! The resurrection sheds light and meaning on the whole Christian mystery. It confers authenticity to the gospels and stimulates hope in the Christian. Paul the Apostle puts it crystal clear: "...and if Christ has not been raised, then our preaching is without substance, and so is your faith"[2] It is therefore no wonder that, to underscore the importance of Easter, forty whole days are set aside in preparations, and another 50 days set apart after its celebration, culminating at Pentecost.

Easter can be likened to a fine orchestra. It began in the low pitch and accelerated to the heights. It flowed like a well-done symphony through dejection, betrayal, condemnation of the innocent, the falls, the intermittent consolation, brutality of the highest order, ruthlessness through a disappointing "Good Friday" that witnessed the death of the Son of God. The story seemed to terminate in a tragedy but God who holds the key of life and death pulled a stunt. When evil had exhausted its arsenals, God who will never abandon his beloved to death pulled an ace, and death the most dreaded enemy of man and the embodiment of all evil and fear met its waterloo! The disappointment of Good Friday dovetailed to a divine-appointment on that beautiful Sunday morning. When all was down with nothing God was up with something!

At Easter Christ rose from the sepulcher, he broke the chains of death and manifests his paschal victory in the lives of all those who are connected to him through faith.

The resurrection of Christ is an enthronement of hope: A feast of hope and encouragement for all who share in the life of God, who must daily be in combat with the forces of evil and goodness, the city of God and the earthly city, the battle for ascendancy between light and darkness. Easter remains God's victory song to humanity that many are the trial of the just one but from them all the Lord shall deliver him.[3]

---

[2]   1 Corinthians 15:14

It is a reminder to us that at night there are tears but joy comes with dawn. The salvation of the just eventually comes to reality.

The lesson of Easter is such that true love always wins. Evil may thrive for millions of years but in the twinkle of an eye truth and love catch up with it. And since our hope cannot deceive us, then we can shout Alleluia. For in the passion and resurrection of Christ God has rescued and has not let the enemy, the evil one, rejoice over us.[4] Not even death, the most dreaded evil, can overcome those who are in Christ Jesus. Having conquered death, it is most certain that there is no other challenge he cannot overcome in all those who are alive in him.

---

[3]   See Psalm 34:19
[4]   See Psalm 30:1

38

The Universality of Salvation

And Jesus said to him, 'Today salvation has come to this
house, because this man too is a son of Abraham; for the
son of man has come to seek out and save what was lost.'
- Luke 19: 9-10.

Many Christians have their favorite bible passages that inspire them
especially when things are not going quite right. John 3:16 seems loved
by many as it reminds us of God's sacrificial love for humanity. The
New International Version puts it as "For God so loved the world that
He gave his only Son that whoever believes in him may not perish but
may have eternal life." The psalmist re-echoes the same message that
God loves all his creatures.[1] Jesus the Lord in that encounter with the
Syro-phoenician woman in desperate need of healing for her son in
spite of the seeming initial reluctance, eventually granted the request

---

[1]   See Psalm 145:9

of a so-called pagan.[2] Even when the Samaritan at Jacob's well drew a line of demarcation and discrimination, reminding the Lord that "Jews do not associate with Samaritans", Jesus did not yield to that blackmail. He went ahead to offer her salvation.[3] In another instance Jesus praised a Roman centurion's faith affirming that "not even in Israel have I found faith as great as this."[4] These and many more are pointers to the fact that the Lord's salvation is meant for all and sundry; that salvation is achievable by all who are connected to him in faith. Christ died for all and his salvation is open to all.

Theologians and mystics have understood the tearing into halves of the Jerusalem Temple Covering to be indicative of a new dawn, the destruction of the man-made barrier between Jews and Gentiles, Greeks and proselytes. Little wonder then that Paul says "There can be neither Jew nor Greek, there can be neither slave nor freeman, there can be neither male nor female – for you are all one in Christ Jesus."[5] It is the same conclusion of the universal availability of the gospel message that Paul made in his dialogue with the Romans and the Jews, "You must realize, then, that this salvation of God has been sent to the gentiles too and they will listen to it."[6] Such is God's plan for humanity to save all things in Christ.

Of all the four evangelists, Luke, possibly owing to his own background, seems the most consistent to portray the universality of God's salvation, and to present Jesus as the savior of all. His presentation of that rather dramatic conversion story of Zacchaeus is indicative of this.[7] Luke uses many elements within this story to depict the story of humanity in search for truth and in need of conversion, contrition and "restitution" for wrongs done to destabilize the order. The curiosity of

---

2   See Mark 7: 24-30
3   See John 4: 1-26
4   Luke 7:9
5   Galatians 3:28
6   Acts of Apostles 28:28
7   See Luke 19: 1-10

Zacchaeus to catch a glimpse of Jesus has many implications for the offer of God's salvation. Though Zacchaeus was rich albeit fraudulently, yet he was poor, for deep within him he felt a hollow that his wealth could not fill. So, he was ready to go to any length to court the friendship of the acclaimed "messiah."

Jesus satisfied the curiosity of Zacchaeus beyond what he could believe. His effort to see Jesus was handsomely rewarded by the Lord who eventually went to sup with him. And like a perfect teacher Jesus used the opportunity of the murmurings of the "crowd" to pass across his salvation-plan for all. He tells them, "Today salvation has come to this house, because this man too is a son of Abraham; for the Son of man has come to seek out and save what was lost"[8]

If God's eternal plan is to save the whole world who are we to sit in judgment like that crowd in Zacchaeus' case? Since he created nothing for damnation, is it not certain that he will have a plan known to him how to save his world? He is ready to save all who are open to his offer of salvation irrespective of whether it makes sense to us or not. God is God, he is no man, and he cannot be boxed to a corner. Even though He works through the ordinary to save (namely the Church and the sacraments), his offer of salvation may not exclude the extra-ordinary means. His salvation encompasses all of his creatures.

---

[8] Luke 19:10

I Believe in the Communion of Saints

Oh when the saints, go marching in,
Oh when the saints go marching in
O Lord I want to be in their number;
Oh when the saints go marching in.

A devoted Christian mother after returning from the morning Mass celebrating the Solemnity of All Saints turned to her eight year old boy and asked, "would you like to be a saint?" He promptly responded saying, "I don't intend being a priest!" Such is one of the many conceptions about sainthood in the Christian world.

Sainthood is not an exclusive of a few. Every November 1st the Church celebrates the Solemnity of All the Saints, known and unknown, especially the canonized, that is those whose sanctity of life is approved and put forward for emulation and intercession by the

Church. The feast of All Saints, among other things, is a reminder of our common vocation to holiness: "Be holy for I the Lord your God I am holy".[1] It is also an apt reminder of our common destiny to be with God at the end of it all in the beatific vision. As Pope Francis puts it, the Saints are those who never lost focus of their vocation.[2] Their faith powered their hope towards its object, love who is God. To the saints, the love of the Lord is better than life.[3]

The saints are those who did battle with the world and with themselves and are victorious. They are victors. The Book of Revelation says of them, "who are these people, dressed in white robes, and where have they come from?... These are the people who have been through the great trial; they have washed their robes white again in the blood of the Lamb. That is why they are standing in front of God's throne and serving him day and night in his sanctuary."[4]

The saints wear the crown of victory now because they had lived out the beatitudes – feeding the hungry, giving water to the thirsty, clothing the naked, sheltering the homeless poor, visiting the sick and prisoner. It is not so much of the big feats they achieved but the much love they put in the little they were able to do in the lord's name. Faithfulness in the little things of life earned them the crown of life, for "a little thing is a little thing but faithfulness in little things is a great thing"[5]

St. Augustine, commenting on the prayer *Our Father*, reminds us of our relationship to the saints when we do say "your kingdom come". In those words we are expressing our desire to be caught up in the destiny of the saints. "This it is that thou dost long for;

---

1   See Leviticus 19:2; 1 Peter 1:16, *Lumen Gentium*, chapter V.
2   Pope Francis, Homily on the Solemnity of All Saints, November 1, 2013.
3   Psalm 63:3.
4   Revelation 7: 13-15.
5   Alfred Broomhall, *Hudson Taylor and China's Open Century*, Book Four: Survivors' Pact. (London: Hodder and Stoughton, 1984), p.154.

this desire in thy prayer, that thou mayest so live, that you mayest have a part in the kingdom of God, which is to be given to all saints. Therefore when thou dost say, "Thy kingdom come", thou dost pray for thyself, that thou mayest live well. Let us have part in Thy kingdom: let that come even to us, which is to come to Thy saints and righteous ones."[6] We share a common destiny with the saints for where we are they once were, and where they are we ought to be and are invited to be. To reach their present abode, the "Blessed Rules" of the beatitudes must be followed with utmost love.[7] To enjoy the blessedness of the saints we must not look to the big shots but pay attention to the seeming inconsequential ordinary things and events with pure love of God.

The Saints, our heroes and heroines of faith were not necessarily people with no history of sin, but people who had the right attitude to sin. They fall rarely but rise promptly. And they did their little, ordinary parts in extraordinary ways. St. Theresa of the Little Flowers for instance remains one of the most astounding saints who teach us the value of the "little" as the key to sainthood. Blessed Theresa of Calcutta teaches us the same lesson with her charism with the poorest of the poor in India. Associating in love with the little brings exaltation. The little, gradual steps of the saints have taken them eventually to the mountain of God, in eternal happiness. Those little, gradual steps are expected of us if we are to join them in the kingdom of eternal joy which lasts forever.

---

[6]   Philip Schaff, ed., *A Select Library of the Nicene and Post-Nicene Fathers of the Christian Church*, Vol. VI, *Saint Augustine: Sermon on the Mount, Harmony of the Gospels, Homilies on the Gospels*, (Grand Rapids: Eerdmans Publishing Company, 1887), P. 276.

[7]   See Matthew 5: 3-10

40

The Widow's Mite

Giving is the highest expression of potency

– Erich Fromm

There is a famous story of a village which once suffered a terrible famine. People hoarded their food and hid it from neighbours and friends. One day, a foreigner arrived in the village, all hungry and disheveled. He went from door to door looking for someone to receive him and for something to eat. One after the other, the villagers told him they too were starving and so could not help him.

It was not until he reached the last house in the village that the poor woman who lived there told the foreigner that all she had left was water but he was welcome to share the water. He said that was more than enough. Then he told her that he had a magic stone with which he could make enough soup to feed the whole village. The starving old woman was excited and went to alert her neighbours. The stranger filled a large pot with the water and threw a round shiny stone into it.

Villagers supplied the firewood and surrounded the large cooking pot to see the miracle of the stone soup.

The stone soup cooked and the hungry villages waited. Then the stranger tasted the cooking soup and said loudly, "Ah! I love this stone soup. Of course, stone soup with a little cabbage is hard to beat." Soon a villager approached hesitantly, holding a cabbage he had retrieved from its hiding place. He gave it to the stranger to add to the pot. "Wonderful!" cried the stranger, "I once had some stone soup with cabbage which had some onions in it that made it fit for a king!" Soon a second villager appeared with some onions and garlic for the soup. On and on he went, through "If only we had a few potatoes.... How wonderful it might be with a couple of carrots" and so on. At last, there was a delicious meal for all. The morale of the story: there is so much potency in the little we all give.

A small mustard seed can grow to be the biggest of all shrubs. A little chuckle with love can save a suicide-bound life. A little kindness of "how are you today" may be the cure for a depressed soul. That is why the Christian worthy of the name cannot hesitate to give of that little to the community in which he or she is found. Little show and share of love here and there can rescue our world from the ravine of individualism it now finds itself. The man who built a mansion began with a stone, goes a Chinese proverb.

Jesus so valued the beauty inherent in the "little" that he presented a little child as the model for those aspiring for heaven. Elijah the great Prophet of Israel was saved from untimely death from the famine he had brought upon Israel by the little and, in fact, the last ounce of bread and litre of oil of the Widow of Zarephath.[1] Another widow in the Gospel won the heart of Christ when she gave her little coins into the treasury.[2]

---

[1]   1 Kings 17: 7-16
[2]   Luke 21: 1-4

The Gospel of John contains that beautiful lesson on not hoarding "the little" which the good Lord, the giver of all good gifts has put at our disposal. Jesus had gone at a full length teaching the multitude who came to him in the desert. He fed them with much spiritual food with his gracious words. But he did not only care about their Spirit; he was equally concerned about their material need; he was concerned about satisfying their need of physical food. So he asked his disciples for a solution. They in turn gave a very human and realistic response telling him to send the people to a neighboring town as it was getting dark. It was far away from town, over five thousand men to feed, and only five loaves of bread and two pieces of fish were available! Yet Jesus gave the command to sit the crowd of people on the lush green and to share the seeming "little" five loaves and the two pieces of fish. Those same five loaves and two fish fed five thousand men, not counting the women who probably even outnumbered the men. He blessed the little and shared. The result was a miracle of the multiplication of loaves. It is God's way to multiply and increase the little in us provided we trust enough to surrender all.

He is still very much able to accept and bless our little efforts at doing the best we can to upturn the reign of sin, to establish the reign of God in our own little ways in whatever capacity we find ourselves. Doing the little is to do our best and never be discouraged to stand for righteousness and truth even if it means standing alone. Your little is important, and so is mine, for put together "the littles" will become an enviable great when handed over to God in love.

The beauty of "the little" is that when shared with love it multiplies! The beauty of 'the little' is in the sharing!

EPILOGUE

Spirited to go on

These reflections, I do hope, have provided reasons why the Word of God is indeed a strong tower.[1] Having gone through diverse forty themes in the ever-satiating fountain of the scriptures, it is pertinent to ask ourselves some important questions and make some necessary personal adjustment. The Word of God always calls to action. Surely these actions differ from an individual to the other, but the presence of the Holy Spirit who is the giver of life and who breaks the Word into its illuminating parts ensures that each person profits from the life communicated in the Word of God.

The question which the individual is prompted to ask, as inspired by the Holy Spirit is: "what is the Word of God asking of me in my particular situation of life? In what way am I to appropriate this Word in such a manner that I bear fruits not only of adoration of God but also of deep wonder at myself?"[2] In what way am I challenged to action by the Word and what shall my response be? It is only in an appropriation of the Word and in the constant struggle of nearness to the person of the Word, Christ himself, that the human person fully comprehends himself or herself.

---

[1] Proverbs 18:10, King James Version.
[2] John Paul II, *Redemptor Hominis*, 10, 1979.

125

Apart from this personal reflection and concern, there is also the preoccupation which comes from without. The fact of the numerous undesirable situations in our world is undeniable. The human person who, according to Irenaeus is created for joy and created to be fully alive, sometimes finds himself divided and under the weight of sin, joylessness and emptiness. Under such situation, Christians who are called to be the light of the world and salt of the earth find it difficult to respond to such a call even in their own lives, how much less in the lives of others. The light is not seen, the salt becomes insipid. Yet the joy of Christ inheres in his Word always, calling us to a rediscovery of that obscured light, and to a rediscovery of that lost taste of life.

Returning to the fount of the Word always refreshes our being helping us to see the world in proper perspective, since indeed *in His light we see light*.[3] Pope Francis, in the opening statement of his first Apostolic Exhortation reminds us that, "the joy of the gospel fills the hearts and lives of all who encounter Jesus. Those who accept his offer of salvation are set free from sin, sorrow, inner emptiness and loneliness. With Christ joy is *constantly* born anew."[4]

The gospel is therefore essentially about joy, for Christ has come to give life and to make us live abundantly.[5] This joy is a dynamic one, one which is constantly sought, appropriated and lived in the course of life with its winding paths. The personal encounter of Christ in the wealth of the scriptures urges us on. He speaks to our heart, making it "burn within us" and helping us to see that no trouble in life can resist the force of the insurmountable hope and strength which comes from the dynamism of his Word.

May that Word enlighten us always, but especially when it appears dark and dreary. May we too be able to ask the Lord, the

---

[3]   Psalm 36:9
[4]   Pope Francis, Apostolic Exhortation *Evangelii Gaudium*, on the proclamation of the gospel in today's world, see www.vatican.va, emphasis mine.
[5]   John 10:10

Word of God, to stay with us *when night approaches* and situations seem incomprehensible, just like it was for the disciples on the way to Emmaus. May we discover, again and again, that joy which shines forth in the presence of the Word.

SUGGESTED FURTHER STUDY

Archbishop Fulton Sheen, *The Eucharist, Audio Book on CD*, Greenville, Texas: Casscom Media, 2013.

Christoph Cardinal Schonborn, *My Jesus: Encountering Christ in the Gospel*, San Francisco: Ignatius Press, 2005.

Hans Urs Von Balthasar and Joseph Cardinal Ratzinger, *Mary, the Church at the Source*, Rome: Libreria Editrice Vaticana, 1997.

John Paul II, *Crossing the Threshold of Hope*, New York: Alfred Knopf Inc., 1994.

John Paul II, *Familiaris Consortio, On the role of the Christian Family in the modern world*, available on www.vatican.va

Pope Francis, *The Joy of the Gospel: Evangelium Gaudium*, Apostolic exhortation available on www.vatican.va.

Saint Augustine, *Confessions*, New York: Oxford University Press, 1991.

Scott Hann, *A Father Who Keeps His Promises: God's Covenant Love in Scripture*, Cincinnati, OH: Servant Books, 1998.

Scott Hann, *Understanding the Scriptures: A Complete Course of Bible Study* Downers Grove, IL: Midwest theological Forum, 2005.

Timothy Keller, *The Prodigal God, Recovering the Heart of the Christian Faith*, New York: Penguin 2008.

Thomas Dubay S.M., *Authenticity: A Biblical Theology of Discernment*, San Francisco: Ignatius Press, 1997.

Scripture Index

132